Basic Needlepoint

BY SANDRA LEY

GROSSET
GOOD LIFE
BOOKS

PUBLISHERS • GROSSET & DUNLAP • NEW YORK

A FILMWAYS COMPANY

Copyright © 1977 by Grosset & Dunlap, Inc.
All rights reserved
Published simultaneously in Canada
Library of Congress catalog card number: 76–15711
ISBN 0-448-12647-8 (trade edition)
ISBN 0-448-13406-3 (library edition)
First printing 1977
Printed in the United States of America

Dedication

To my colleagues in the craft field whose devotion to their work supercedes all other considerations. And special thanks to Mr. Emil Wurio, President, D.M.C. Corporation.

Contents

Introduction

The form of needlework now called "needlepoint" has existed in various cultures for thousands of years. It can be seen in some remnants of textiles found in the tombs of the Egyptian pharaohs. It wasn't until the invention of the metal needle in the sixteenth century that needlepoint really became popular. The Elizabethans used needlepoint to make table carpets (the floors were covered with rushes and dried grasses), which were imitations of very rare ones they had imported from the East.

Needlepoint has gained and lost in popularity since Elizabethan times. It became so popular in the second half of the last century that for a while it looked as if all other forms of embroidery would be abandoned. But from the turn of the century until about ten years ago, other forms of needlework replaced needlepoint in everyday use. Then modern women (and men) turned to it again, this time using it as an expression of modern creativity. This form of needlework has never had as many adherents as it does today.

The heavy designs of the nineteenth century have been replaced by contemporary designs, which are limited only by the designer's imagination. Inspirations for needlepoint designs can be found everywhere, and once you have acquired the basic materials and have mastered a few basic stitches (which will not take you long), you will soon be designing and making your own masterpieces. These masterpieces will give great pleasure to you, your family, and your friends. And someday they may even wind up in a museum as superb examples of the great needlepoint renaissance of the last half of the twentieth century.

Perhaps you want to start a needlepoint project, but because of the profusion of canvases and yarns available, you simply don't know where to begin. You may have looked at prepackaged kits and have been disappointed at the poor and unimaginative designs available. And if your town has a store that sells very well designed canvases, they may be so expensive that you don't want to buy them because you don't know whether a beginner's stitches could do them justice.

You may have seen for sale in some needlepoint stores canvases with the design already worked and the background left blank for you to fill in. You are right in not buying preworked canvas. Working the background of an already finished design is the most boring thing I can think of and may put you off for life.

If any of the above have stopped you from beginning what can be a delightful and rewarding hobby, you no longer have to be stopped by these obstacles. This book will show you how to adapt your own designs and how to buy everything you will need to make beautiful things for yourself, your home, and your friends at a fraction of the cost of kits or pre-painted canvases. The confusing selection of canvases, yarns, and accessories will be explained so that you can walk into any needlework or department store and buy only what you need for the work you want to do. Needlepoint is one hobby that can be as inexpensive or as expensive as you want it to be.

In addition to the basic needlepoint stitches you will learn a great many other stitches, enabling you to create completely original masterpieces. You can start your new hobby with one of the simple projects in this book, and it won't be long before you will have the confidence to branch out on your own designs (although there are so many delightful projects in this book, you will probably want to make several of them).

Needlepoint is a neat, clean hobby with nothing to spill. It is also a very portable hobby (unless you become so expert and inspired that you want to make rugs), which can be folded up and taken with you almost anywhere and can be worked on in almost all surroundings. The time we all spend traveling, waiting for dentists, watching television, or chatting with friends also can be used to work on your creation. One warning: needlepoint is habit forming. Once you start you might not want to stop, and you will probably plan your next project while you are halfway through the first one.

Start by reading the entire book, and then with needle in hand, you will soon be involved in the beautiful world of needlepoint. It's not difficult, and you'll soon be wondering how you ever were able simply to sit around without keeping your hands busy.

1
What You Need to Start

Needlepoint is not an expensive hobby, but there are several basic things you need to begin.

Canvases

The first thing you need is canvas. All needlepoint is worked on stiff fabric woven with open meshes between the threads. This canvas is available in different widths and is sold by the yard like fabric. It can be purchased from needlepoint stores, the needlework department of large stores, and mail-order supply houses. Many stores, particularly the mail-order houses, will not sell less than one yard of canvas; but in the long run, this is the most economical way to buy it, since you can make several projects from that one yard. The number of projects obtained from one yard of canvas depends on the width of the canvas and, of course, on the size of your projects. Even little pieces of canvas left over from large projects can be used to make small items, such as the bookmarks and holiday ornaments in the Needlepoint Projects chapter of this book.

The two most important things to look for when buying canvas are quality and mesh size (the number of intersecting threads per inch). There is no point in wasting time and money on inferior canvas. The best canvas is evenly woven and must not have any knotted, thin, or distorted threads. Examine the piece you are buying very carefully to be sure that the threads are at perfect right angles to each other. Refuse to buy any canvas that has little knots tied in the threads; you cannot do needlepoint stitches over knots in the canvas, but the worst thing about the knots is that they may pull out when the canvas is blocked, ruining everything.

With few exceptions good canvas is very stiff when new, though it will soften as you work on it. Some European and petit point canvases are soft to begin with, but this in no way makes them inferior. Have no fear about the quality of the canvas you will get from a mail-order supply house (which is often the most economical place to buy it). The store's reputation depends on the high quality of its merchandise, and it will accept returns in the rare instances when they

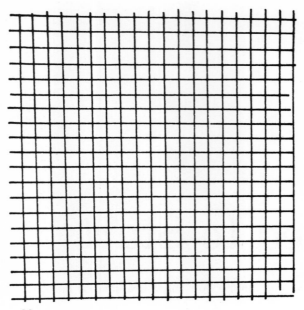

Mono canvas

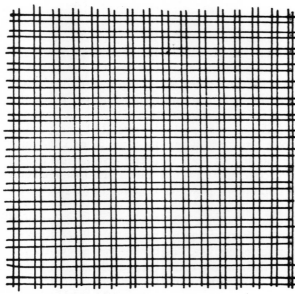

Penelope or duo canvas

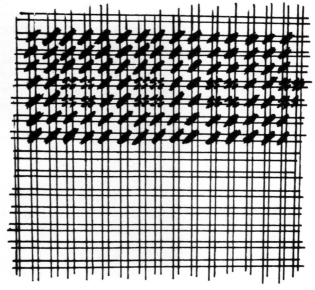

Stitches on penelope canvas

are necessary. Avoid buying needlepoint canvas in bargain basements or variety stores. Much of the canvas sold in these stores is not worth working with.

There are two basic kinds of canvas: mono (single thread) and penelope or duo (double thread). Mono canvas is the most popular and the easiest for the beginner to work with, since the threads can be seen and counted easily. The advantage of penelope canvas is that the double threads can be divided so that two different size stitches can be used on the same piece of canvas. Penelope canvas can be used as if it were mono canvas without dividing the threads. For the half cross-stitch (see page 24) penelope canvas is essential, since the threads of the mono canvas are not sturdy enough to support this stitch.

Canvas is classified according to mesh size. The fewer threads there are to the inch, the larger the finished stitch will be. For most needlepoint 10-mesh canvas is the most convenient. Work done on 10- or 12-mesh canvas is often referred to as gros point, or large stitch. Petit point, or small stitch, work is done on 16- to 18-mesh canvas and is not recommended for the beginner. These fine-mesh canvases are used for very intricate designs with a great deal of color shading.

The most popular size of penelope canvas is 10/20, which means that there will be 10 large

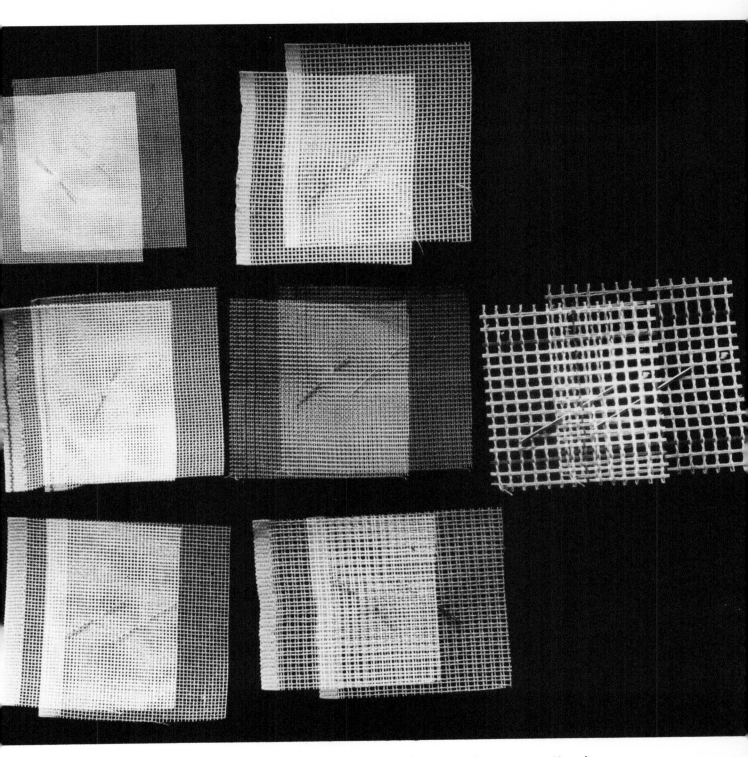

Various sizes of canvas shown with the appropriate size needles. Starting in the upper left hand corner and going from top to bottom: Petite point (18 mesh) canvas; 14 mesh mono canvas; 12 mesh mono canvas; 10 mesh mono canvas; 10/20 penelope canvas; 5 mesh rug canvas; 3½ mesh rug canvas.

stitches to the inch while the thread can be separated to work 20 stitches to the inch.

Rug canvas is a form of double-thread canvas that can be used with heavy yarn. Such needlepoint is called "quick point." Rug canvas comes in 3½ and 5 meshes to the inch. It is ideal for working quick projects (such as the Rose Pillow Project on page 61) and is easy for beginners and children to use. Do not try to separate the double threads of the rug canvas, since they do not work the same way as penelope canvas.

Bargello canvas is made for Bargello or Florentine stitching (see page 34) and usually comes 13 meshes to the inch. Bargello work is composed of upright (not slanting) stitches that cover two or more meshes of the canvas. By moving up or down one or two meshes for each stitch, repeating geometric patterns are formed. (You cannot make pictures with Bargello as you can with regular needlepoint.) Many beautiful Bargello patterns are made by using several shades of the same color. Although Bargello can be done on penelope canvas, mono canvas is preferable, since it is easier to count the threads of the canvas.

A plastic form of "canvas" has been introduced in the last few years and is used in kits to make handbags and other small projects. It is sold in square or rectangular sheets and in small modules (various geometric shapes) that can be pieced together like patchwork. The plastic remains very stiff and can really only be used for such things as book covers and the aforementioned handbags. And since the use of plastic is extremely limited, I prefer to do needlepoint on a fabric canvas.

Interlock canvas is a specially woven mono canvas that keeps its shape better than regular canvas. It comes in the same sizes as other mono canvases and is used in the same way.

Interlock canvas is white. Petit point canvas is white or pale yellow, and penelope canvas is an antique beige color. Some canvases come with red or blue lines woven in at periodic intervals; these lines are used as a guide for counting stitches when working from a graph or on a pattern design. These lines and the color of the canvas are completely covered by the stitches when the work is finished, so don't be concerned if you are working with a light-colored yarn on a yellow or beige canvas.

Yarns

The mesh of your canvas determines the kind of yarn to be used, although this can be very flexible.

Persian yarn: Persian yarn is a slightly hairy woolen yarn. It comes in 3 ply, which means that it is made up of three threads wound around each other. This yarn can be used as it comes on 10-mesh canvas or can be separated into two-ply thread for working on 12- through 16-mesh canvas. Single strands of Persian yarn can be used for petit point on high-count canvases.

Persian yarn is sold in two ways: in precut strands by the ounce or pound or in skeins of about 8 or 40 yards. Some needlework stores let you buy as little as one strand of a color, if that is all you need.

Tapestry yarn: Tapestry yarn is slightly heavier than three-ply Persian yarn and has a soft, nonhairy texture. It is ideal for gros point work. Although tapestry yarn is also made of several plys of thread, it does not separate easily and should be used as it comes. Tapestry yarn comes in skeins of differing yardage, depending on the manufacturer. Check the packaging for length.

Matte cotton embroidery thread: Matte cotton embroidery thread has a dull texture. It comes from France and is seldom used for needlepoint in this country. This is sad, since the colors are beautiful and the thread is delightfully soft to work with. The only way I know of to buy this thread is to order it from the manufacturer, D.M.C. Corporation (see address on page 93), which sells it in small skeins. It can be used with 10-, 12- and 14-mesh canvas. It is perfect for those people who are allergic to wool and is a much better substitute for wool than synthetic yarns.

Embroidery floss: Embroidery floss comes in a 6-strand ply that can be separated and used on canvases of many different mesh sizes, depending on the number of strands used together. It is best used as a color accent with a woolen yarn, since the thread has an almost

Needlepoint yarns. From left to right: rug yarn (woolen); tapestry yarn; Persian yarn; pearl cotton; matte cotton; embroidery floss.

silklike sheen — and it is cheaper and easier to work with than real silk. It is also possible to make small needlepoint projects entirely out of embroidery floss. The range of colors available is enormous, making it possible to make needlepoint miniatures of works of art.

Silk floss: Silk floss looks like cotton floss and can be used in the same way, although it is tricky to work with. In needlepoint, the thread sometimes catches on the canvas and has to be worked very carefully. It is a good idea to run the thread over dressmaker's beeswax to make it smoother before using it. Silk floss is sold in exclusive boutiques and is very expensive. Use it for accents in combination with wool.

Pearl embroidery thread: Size-5 pearl embroidery thread can be doubled and used on 14-mesh canvas to give an interesting, slightly shiny effect. It is sold in little balls with about 50 yards of thread on each ball. The color range is quite extensive.

Yarns to Avoid

Yarns meant for knitting are not suitable for needlepoint. Needlepoint yarn is stronger and less stretchy than knitting yarn. Knitting yarn will not cover the canvas evenly and will wear thin as the needle passes through the holes of the canvas over and over again.

Some kits include synthetic yarns (usually acrylic) for needlepoint. Stay away from them, even in the smallest amounts. They look fine as you work on them, but very soon your pillow or other project will pill and form small balls of fluff, which destroy the effect of the needlepoint, and there is nothing you can do to remedy the situation.

Check the label, when buying a needlepoint kit. It should tell you whether the yarn in the kit is all wool, synthetic, or a combination of both. Do not buy yarns for needlepoint if they are not labeled as to fiber content. All good needlepoint yarns are made of natural fibers.

How Much Will You Need?

The amount of yarn or thread you will need for a project depends on the size of the canvas and the type of stitch you will be working in. To estimate this amount, work a measured amount over the size of the canvas you will be using in the stitch you will be working in until you have completed one square inch. Multiply the amount of yarn used by the finished size of the canvas. Buy enough yarn at one time to complete the project, since dye lots can vary. There is nothing more frustrating than being three yards short of the color needed to finish a project. It is always better to buy a little more yarn than you think you will need. The leftover colors can be used later for small projects.

When working a design that calls for small amounts of many different colors use your judgment about how much of each color yarn you will need. After you have completed a couple of projects you will have developed a sense of how much yarn you need to fill in these small areas. For a beginning project it's best to ask the salesperson when you buy the yarn. Remember that the amount of yarn needed also depends on the stitch you plan to use. For example, the continental and basketweave stitches use twice as much yarn as the half cross-stitch because they completely cover the back of the canvas as well as the front.

Needles

Blunt-tipped tapestry needles are used for needlepoint. The size of the needle you need depends on the size of your canvas. The smallest needle sizes, #24 and #22, are used on 18-, 16-, and 14-mesh canvas. The next size, #20, is for 12- and 10-mesh canvas. And the most often used size, #18, is used on 10-mesh canvas. Rug canvases require a size #13 rug needle, which is just like a large tapestry needle.

The best way to determine if your needle is the right size is to pass it through one of the holes in the canvas. It should pass through easily without pushing the threads aside. The eye of the needle should also be large enough to accommodate your yarn. This will not be a problem if the yarn is the right size for the canvas you are using.

Scissors. From left to right: dressmaker's shears, embroidery scissors; stork-shaped needlepoint scissor and the ever-useful thimble.

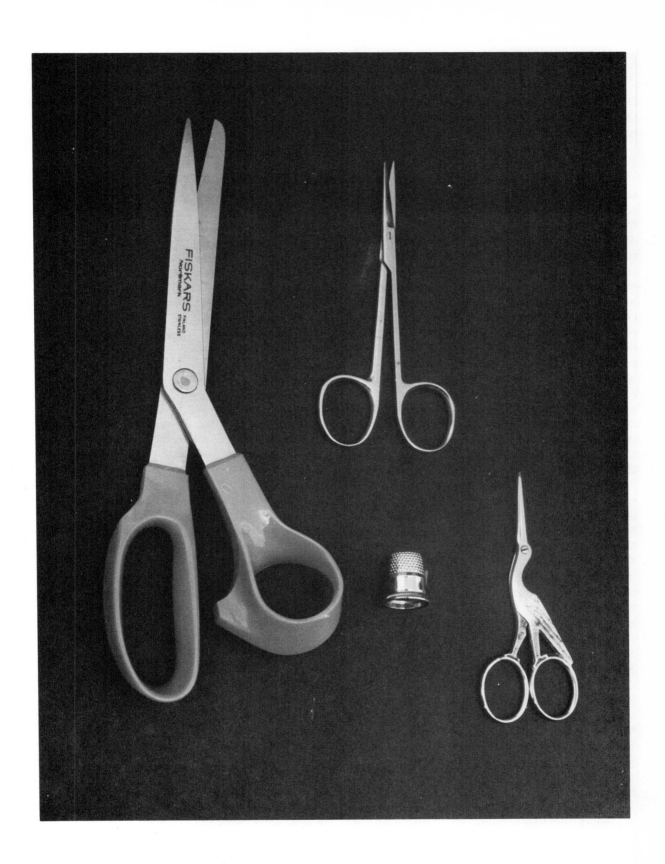

Other Needlepoint Equipment

There are several other things you are likely to need to do needlepoint projects. Some of them are not absolutely necessary, but they are nice to have.

Frames

There are two schools of thought about the necessity of needlepoint frames. Some experts say that all needlepoint should be done on a frame to prevent the canvas from becoming distorted. But the frames are awkward and make your needlepoint a stationary hobby rather than a portable one. Without a frame you can always roll up your needlepoint canvas and carry it with you. Any distortion in the canvas will be corrected by blocking after the project is finished. The only time a frame is necessary is when you are working on an extremely large canvas, where the weight of the work will be too heavy to support on your lap comfortably. It's not likely that you'd carry such a large project around anyway.

Some people recommend placing the canvas in an embroidery hoop. I am entirely opposed to this idea, since the hoop can actually break the threads of the canvas.

If you do want to try using a frame, the most comfortable ones to work with come with rollers. The canvas is attached to the rollers at the top and bottom, and the work is then rolled so that only the area being worked on is exposed. These frames come in different widths and must be slightly larger than the width of the piece you are working with. They can be purchased in the same places that you buy canvas. Some very good ones are available from the mail-order houses.

Masking Tape

Use masking tape to cover the edges of the canvas. This is necessary for two reasons: First, the canvas unravels at the edges if it is not taped; second, the rough edges of untaped canvas catch the yarn and damage it every time you take a stitch.

Scissors

You will need two types of scissors. Use dressmaking shears to cut the canvas. Use embroidery or needlepoint scissors to cut the strands of yarn to working size, to trim off any "tails" of yarn hanging out at the back when you start or end a length of yarn, and if absolutely necessary, to cut out mistakes.

Marking Pens

Marking pens are essential for transferring the design to the canvas. They *must* be waterproof. The best pens are marked permanent, waterproof, and smearproof. If you have any doubts about the pen you want to use, cut out a small piece of canvas (about 2 inches by 2 inches) and make two crisscrossing lines on the canvas. Let the ink dry thoroughly and soak the canvas in cold water for a few minutes. If it washes off or smears, *don't* use that pen. There are few things as disappointing as finishing a beautiful piece of needlepoint only to have ink from the marking lines leak through and stain the yarn during blocking.

Acrylic Paints

If you are going to do your own designs and want to be sure of the color combinations and placement before you start, you consider painting the design on the canvas. Acrylic paints are the best to use, since they can be thinned and they dry very quickly. To paint the design on the canvas, first get out a few newspapers and lay them under the canvas. Trace the outlines of the design on the canvas with a marking pen. Mix the paint in the colors you want and use the medium that comes with the paint to make it quite thin. This is necessary because thick paint will clog up the holes of the canvas, making it impossible to pull the yarn through. Do not start to work on the needlepoint until the canvas is completely dry. Let the canvas dry for at least 24 hours.

Tracing Paper

Use tracing paper to copy a design (or draw your own) before it is transferred to the canvas. Copy the design with a black marking pen; use a fairly thick line for easy visibility.

Blocking Boards

You need a plywood board larger than the size of your project to block it. A 24- by 26-inch board will suffice for all the projects in this book, but a smaller piece will be handier for the smaller projects.

Rustproof Tacks

Make sure that the tacks you buy for blocking your needlepoint projects are rustproof.

Thimble

Many needlepointers find working with a thimble awkward; however, it is much easier on your fingers if you learn to use a thimble from the beginning. You don't have to have a fancy antique thimble; you can buy a perfectly good one in a sewing supply or variety store. Make sure that it is small enough to fit comfortably without pinching and without falling off. Buy more than one; thimbles have an amazing habit of getting permanently lost.

Tweezers

Unless you have long fingernails, this little tool will come in handy to grasp and remove threads when correcting mistakes.

2
Beginning to Needlepoint

Finding and Enlarging Designs

Many designs can be used for needlepoint, even if they are too large or small for the project you want to make. To enlarge a design (either from this book or from some other source), draw a series of equally spaced lines horizontally and then vertically across the design to form a grid. Then, on a clean sheet of paper, draw another grid with the same *number* of squares but making the squares as large as needed for the design to fit your project. For example, if the design is to be four times larger than the original, make each square four times as large as those on the original design. Copy the design from the original square by square.

If you find it difficult (or impossible) to draw a series of parallel lines over the design so that the squares come out even, pick up a few sheets of various-sized grid paper from a needlepoint store or art supply shop. One of the most popular of these premarked papers comes with the grid marked in 1-inch squares. Transfer the lines from the appropriate-sized grid to tracing paper, which can then be laid over the design. The design will show through, and it can be drawn square by square onto a larger grid (premarked or hand-drawn). The enlarged design can then be transferred to canvas.

Designs can be reduced in the same way, by copying a design from a larger grid onto a smaller one.

But, you may ask, where do I find designs? The answer is, practically everywhere (in addition to the ones in this book). Any drawing with sharp, clear outlines will lend itself to needlepoint. This includes greeting cards, book illustrations (especially juvenile picture books), coloring books (both children's and the new sophisticated ones for adults), your or your children's own drawings, art books, magazines, and wallpaper. You can even trace a photograph if you first draw around the outlines of the object with a black marking pen. If you don't want to damage a good photograph, place a piece of tracing paper over the photo and draw the outlines on the tracing paper. I find seed catalogs, with their beautiful color photographs of flowers and fruits, a wonderful source of inspiration.

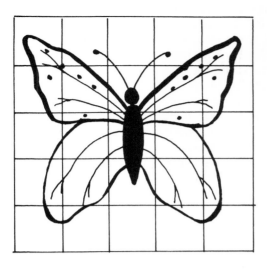

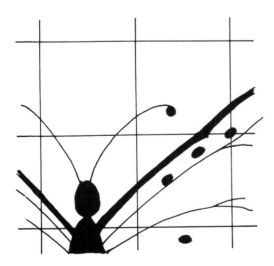

Enlarging a design

Keep your first few projects simple, without small details and large amounts of shading. You will graduate to these after a little practice. There is literally no end to the amount of sources of needlepoint designs. Just keep your eyes open — you're sure to find designs in even more places than mentioned here.

Transferring Designs to Canvas

Once you have found your design and have enlarged it to the proper size, you are ready to transfer it to the canvas. Cut out a piece of the canvas the size of your design and background plus 3 to 4 inches around all four sides. This last is very important, since you need a margin of unworked canvas in order to block the piece properly. Cover the raw edges of the canvas with 1-inch-wide masking tape all the way around (if the canvas selvedge is still on, it is not necessary to tape that edge, since it will not unravel. Hold the selvedge to the side of the work).

Fold the canvas in half and crease it with your hands. Open it up and make a light pencil line along the crease between the threads. Fold it in half the other way, crease it, and make another pencil line at right angles to the first line. The center of the canvas is now marked by the intersecting lines. Place the canvas over your drawing with the center of the canvas at the center of the drawing. Hold the canvas down at all four corners with small, heavy objects (such as paperweights). With a black, waterproof marking pen trace over the lines of the drawing. It may be necessary to lift an edge of the canvas occasionally to see the drawing more clearly. If you are using a fine-mesh canvas (petit point), you may not be able to see the lines of the drawing clearly in which case you will have to use one of the following methods to trace the design.

If you have a glass-topped table, place the drawing and the canvas on the table as described and place a small bright light under the glass top. You will then be able to see the design through the canvas clearly. If such a table is unavailable, wait for a sunny day and tape the drawing with the canvas over it to a win-

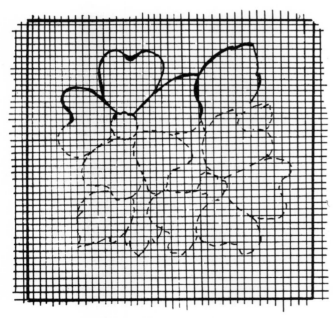

Tracing a design onto canvas

dowpane. The bright sunlight shining through the drawing and the canvas allows the drawing to show clearly through the canvas. The only drawback is that you will have to do your tracing standing up, so if you are working on a large or complicated design, take periodic rests so that your arm and shoulder don't cramp.

After the design has been traced onto the canvas, you can use waterproof markers or acrylic paint to color the canvas so that you don't have to keep referring back to the original for the color placement. Follow the instructions on page 16 for using acrylics to paint the canvas.

Working from Graphs

If you are going to use a design which has been graphed (whether from this book or another source) it is not necessary to trace the design onto the canvas. Each square of the graph represents an *intersecting mesh of the canvas* and the stitches are counted while being worked. The squares of the graph are marked with little symbols. These markings indicate the color of the stitching and are deciphered by a code given with the graph. Cut your canvas to the size called for in the instructions, being sure that you allow for margins all around the piece. Mark the center of the canvas by folding it in half and in half again as described, and start the stitching following the color placement of the graph. Some graphs indicate a starting point; others do not. If a graph does not indicate where to begin, start where it seems easiest for you. Keep the graph in front of you as you work and change the colors accordingly. By the way, once you have learned to work from a graph, it is not necessary to restrict yourself to graphs made especially for needlepoint. Cross-stitch graphs and those used for making crocheted pictures (filet crochet) can be used to make lovely needlepoint. Your only job will be to select the colors you want to use.

How to Do the Stitching

Before you begin to stitch, it may be necessary to prepare the yarn. If the yarn you are using comes in skeins rather than precut

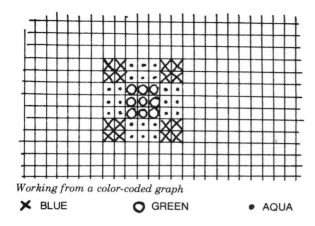

Working from a color-coded graph

✖ BLUE   ⭕ GREEN   ● AQUA

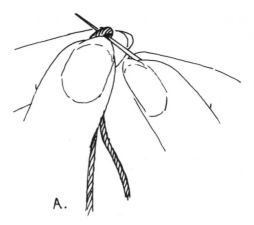

A.

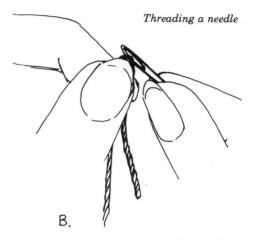

Threading a needle

B.

strands, cut it to workable lengths. Because a strand of yarn experiences a great deal of strain as it is passed through the canvas, it musn't be too long or it will wear thin and/or get snarled up. Cut the yarn into strands 18 to 22 inches long. Place all the strands of one color side by side and tie them into a large, loose knot. Repeat this for each color. Keep the yarn in this loose knot and pull each strand out from the center of the knot. If you are using Persian yarn, embroidery floss or a similar material with plies that will have to be separated, do this as you go along.

Start the stitching with the design; the background should be done later. Do the white or lighter colors of the design first. If you work the dark colors of the design first, the light ones may pick up fibers from the dark ones as you work.

To thread the needle, lay the end of the yarn lightly over the middle of the needle and pinch it together firmly. Still pinching the yarn, remove the needle from under it and pass the pinched end through the eye of the needle. This may seem difficult at first, but after a few practice runs, you will be able to do it without even thinking about it.

To start the first stitch, tie a knot in the end of the yarn. Then insert the needle from the right side of the canvas a few inches away from the area you are going to cover. Bring the needle to the back of the canvas with the knot on top, and bring the needle up from the back of the canvas and make your first stitches. After you have completed several stitches, catching

the beginning long strand of the yarn in the stitching at the back of the canvas, cut off the knot and pull the end of the yarn through to the back of the work. End off your first strand of yarn by weaving about two inches in at the back of the stitches you have made. End off every strand of yarn this way; just be sure not to weave a dark or bright color into a light or white one, since it will show from the front and look dirty.

To start the next strand of yarn, weave it into the back of the stitches you have already made for about an inch and a half and continue stitching. Never tie a knot in the yarn to be left at the back of the work; this would leave lumps in the work that could not be removed later. Make your stitches as even as possible. Pull the yarn through the holes in the canvas gently and never tug at it. It is important to achieve a smooth, even tension. Your work may look a little uneven at first, but it will not be long before you have caught the rhythm of the stitching and your work will acquire the desired even effect. Do not jump the yarn across the back of the work for more than half an inch. If the yarn gets twisted (and it will), drop the needle and hold the canvas up at about eye level. The weight of the hanging needle causes the yarn to untwist naturally. You will probably have to repeat this frequently as you work. If your design calls for small amounts of a color in many different places, cut the yarn and start fresh each time by weaving the yarn into the new area to be worked.

Do all the outlining (straight horizontal and vertical lines, and curved lines) in the continental stitch (see stitch instructions on page 23). To work curved lines, make small "steps," following the outline as closely as possible. Unless you are using stitches other than a tent stitch, fill in the outlines with the continental stitch. Fill in larger areas of color in the design and the background with the basketweave stitch. Always start the background in the upper right-hand corner.

Making Samplers

If you are going to experiment with the decorative stitches, it's best to start by making a sampler. Take a piece of 10-mesh mono canvas and divide it into squares, one square for each stitch you want to use. Make each section about 4 inches square. Work each square in a different stitch in a different color. (For example, follow the instructions given on pages 39–43 for a sampler pillow.) After your sampler is finished, you will have a good idea of how the stitches look when grouped together and you can refer to your sampler when composing your design.

Fixing Mistakes

If you make a mistake, don't panic. Stop stitching immediately. With the embroidery or needlepoint scissors carefully (*very carefully*) cut out each individual stitch. Do this only under a good light and be very sure that you do *not* cut the canvas thread. You will find it easier to make one clip in the back of the stitch and another clip in the front. Once each stitch has been clipped, you can pull the thread out with a pair of tweezers.

If after you have finished an area you discover that one or two stitches have been made in the wrong color, you can correct them without having to cut them out. Simply thread your needle with the right color and make new stitches over the old ones. Be sure that you don't pull the yarn too tight and that the new stitches completely cover the old ones.

When the piece is completely finished, check for missed stitches. The easiest way to do this is to hold the canvas up to a strong light. If you have skipped any stitches you will see obvious holes. Using the color called for in the design, thread the needle and fill in the missed stitches. If you notice what look like holes where there are no missed stitches, it means that you have been pulling too hard on the yarn, especially around the edges of a solid area of color. Don't worry about this, it will be corrected when you block the piece, but remember it for your next project and try to keep your stitching tension more even.

3
The Most Popular Stitches

Tent Stitches

The four stitches that follow are variations of the tent stitch, which is the stitch most often used for needlepoint work. All of these stitches look the same on the right side of the work, but they look quite different on the back.

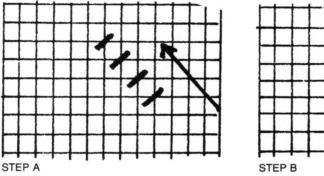 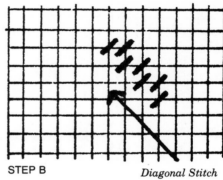

STEP A   STEP B   *Diagonal Stitch*

Diagonal Stitch

The diagonal stitch prevents the canvas from being pulled out of shape. Start at the lower right-hand corner of the canvas. Work all the rows diagonally upward, finishing off at the end of each row.

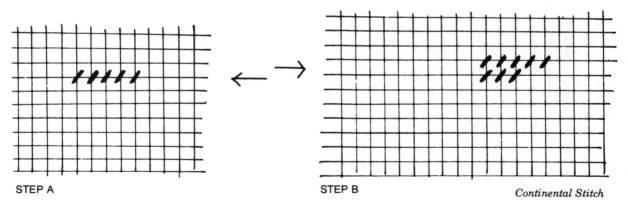

STEP A   ← →   STEP B   *Continental Stitch*

Continental Stitch

The continental stitch is both a background and an outline stitch. Single lines may be worked up or down, sideways and curved, to outline the work. For background, each row of this stitch is worked from right to left or from top to bottom. When working horizontally, the canvas must be turned upside down when a new row is started. Start at the lower right-hand corner; finish the row. To start the next row, invert the canvas and repeat the same procedure as for row one.

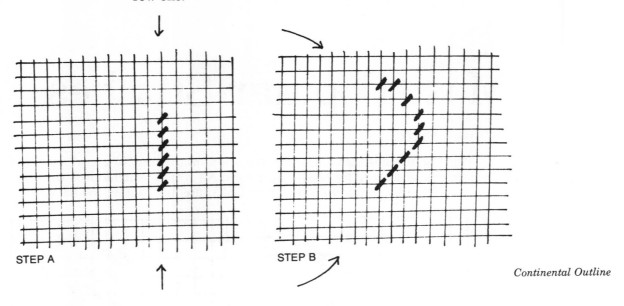

STEP A   STEP B

Continental Outline

Half Cross-stitch

The half cross-stitch uses the least amount of yarn, but it can only be worked successfully on penelope canvas. It is not recommended for any kind of needlepoint that will receive wear, since it is the weakest of the tent stitches.

Start at the top of the canvas. Work all rows from left to right. Invert the canvas at the end of each row. Step B of the illustration shows the first stitch of the second row.

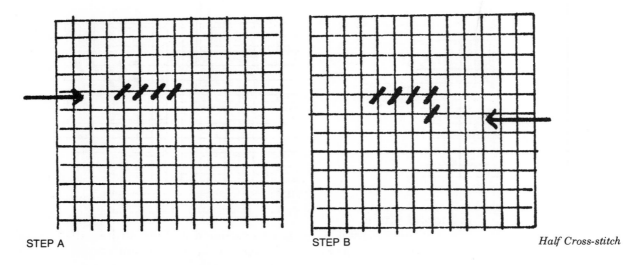

STEP A   STEP B   *Half Cross-stitch*

Basketweave Stitch

The basketweave stitch produces a firm background, and it does not distort the canvas as much as the continental stitch and the half cross-stitch. The canvas is kept upright at all times while working.

Start at the upper right-hand corner of the canvas. Work the rows, alternating upward and downward stitches. Steps A, B, and C show the first, second, and third rows. Repeat steps B and C.

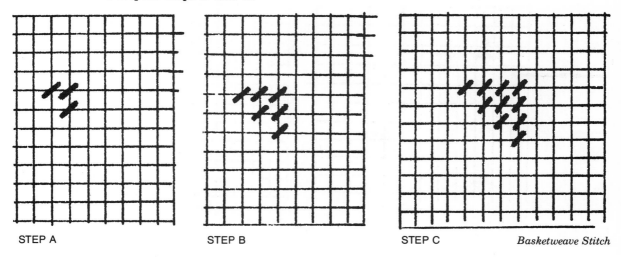

STEP A   STEP B   STEP C   *Basketweave Stitch*

Cross-stitches

Cross-stitch

Start at the top of the canvas. All rows start and end at the left. Step B shows the first stitch of the second row.

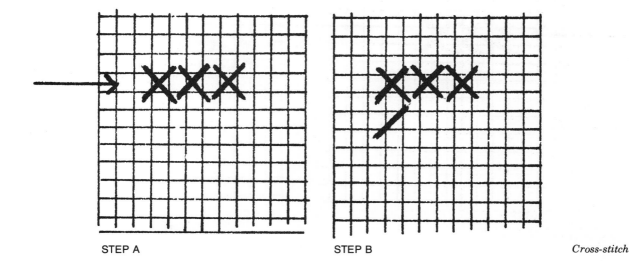

STEP A   STEP B   *Cross-stitch*

Upright Cross-stitch

Start at the top of the canvas and work all the rows from left to right. Turn the canvas upside down at the end of each row. Step B shows the first upright cross-stitch of the second row.

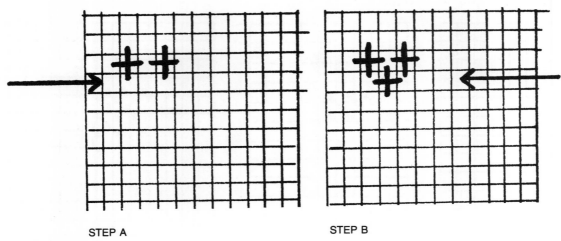

STEP A   STEP B

Upright Cross-stitch

Long-legged Cross-stitch

Start at the top of the canvas and work all the rows from left to right. Step A shows the beginning and ending of a row. Turn the canvas upside down at the end of each row. Step B shows the first stitch of the second row.

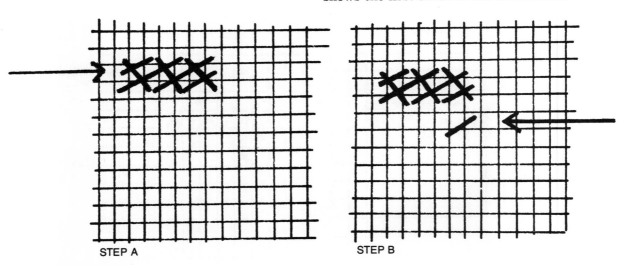

STEP A   STEP B

Long-legged Cross-stitch

Smyrna Cross-stitch

Start at the top or bottom of the canvas and work all the rows from the left to the right, finishing off at the end of each row. Step C shows the first stitch of the second row.

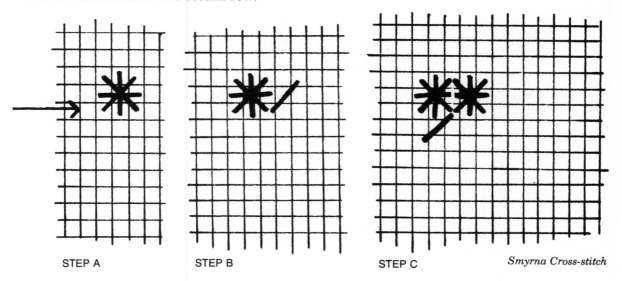

STEP A   STEP B   STEP C   *Smyrna Cross-stitch*

Tramé Cross-stitch

The tramé cross-stitch may be worked with two different colors. Start at the top or the bottom of the canvas. Work the tramé rows first, from right to left. Then work the cross-stitch (as explained above) over the tramé rows with a lighter weight yarn in the same color.

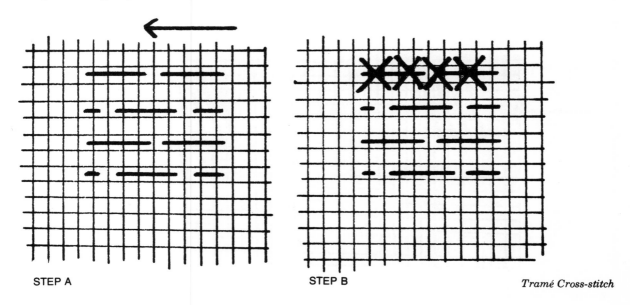

STEP A   STEP B   *Tramé Cross-stitch*

Gobelin Stitches

Upright Gobelin Stitch

The upright Gobelin stitch can be worked over 2 to 6 meshes of the canvas. Start at the top of the canvas and work the first row from left to right. Work the second row from right to left. Step B shows the first stitch of the second row.

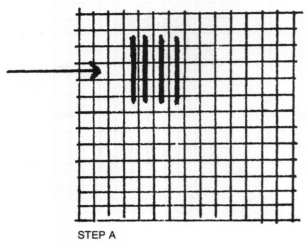

STEP A

STEP B

Upright Gobelin Stitch

Slanting Gobelin Stitch

The slanting Gobelin stitch can be worked over 2 to 6 meshes of the canvas. Start at the top of the canvas and work the first row from left to right. Work the second row from right to left. Step B shows the first stitch of the second row.

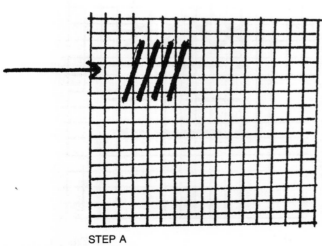
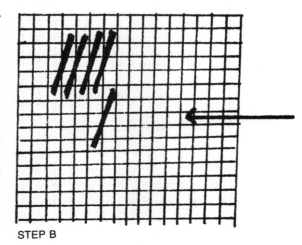

STEP A

STEP B

Slanting Gobelin Stitch

Encroaching Gobelin Stitch

The encroaching Gobelin stitch also can be worked over 2 to 6 meshes of the canvas, as can the other Gobelin stitches. Start at the top of the canvas and work the first row from left to right. Work the second row from right to left. Step B shows the first stitch of the second row.

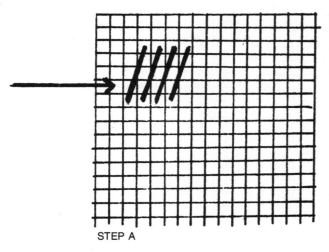

STEP A

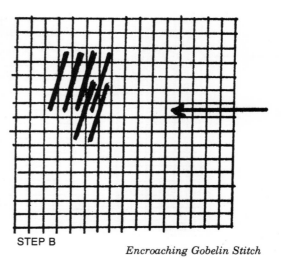

STEP B

Encroaching Gobelin Stitch

Gobelin Stitch Variation

The Gobelin stitch variation is used for Bargello, and each row can be worked in a different color. Start at the center of the canvas and work the first row from the center to the sides. Work the second and even-numbered rows the same way, but working over 2 meshes only (as shown in step B). Work the following rows up toward the top of the canvas. Turn your canvas upside down and work the other half.

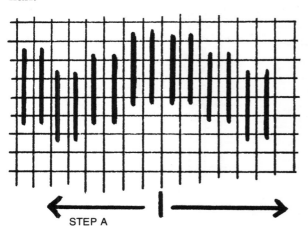

STEP A

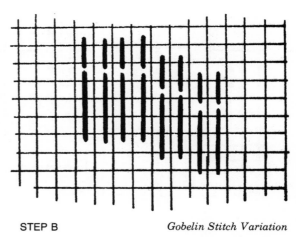

STEP B

Gobelin Stitch Variation

Other Decorative Stitches

Scotch Stitch

Start at the top of the canvas and work all the rows from left to right. Turn the canvas upside down at the end of each row. Step B shows the first stitch of the next square. Step C shows the first stitch of the second row.

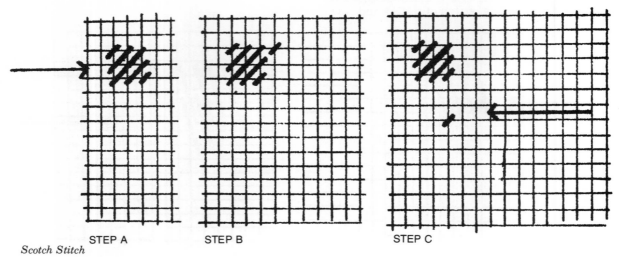

STEP A   STEP B   STEP C

Scotch Stitch

Scotch Stitch Variation

Start at the bottom of the canvas and work the outline of the squares in the half cross-stitch. First complete all the vertical lines; then complete the horizontal lines. Work the center of the squares in the Scotch stitch.

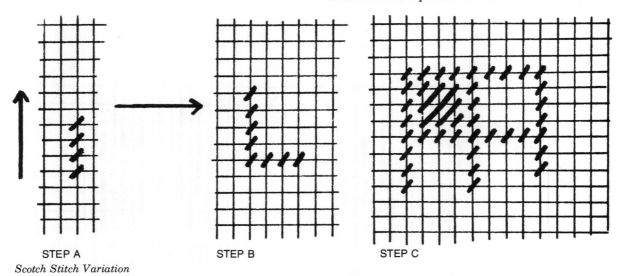

STEP A   STEP B   STEP C

Scotch Stitch Variation

Checkerboard Stitch

Start at the top of the canvas and work all the rows from left to right. Turn the canvas upside down at the end of each row. Step B shows the first stitch of the second row.

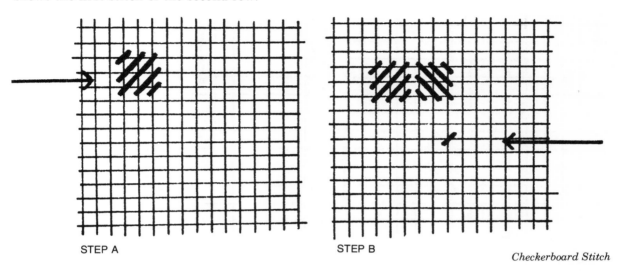

STEP A

STEP B

Checkerboard Stitch

Cashmere Stitch

Start at the bottom of the canvas and work all the rows from right to left. Turn the canvas upside down at the end of each row. Step B shows the first stitch of the next square. Step C shows the first stitch of the second row.

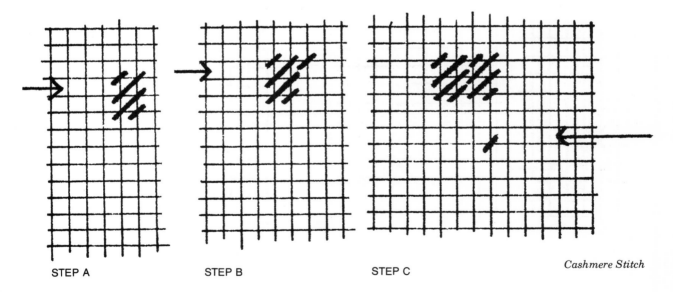

STEP A

STEP B

STEP C

Cashmere Stitch

Cashmere Stitch Variation

Start at the bottom right of the canvas and work in vertical rows. Turn the canvas upside down at the end of each row. Step A shows the beginning and ending of a row, while step B shows the first stitch of the second row.

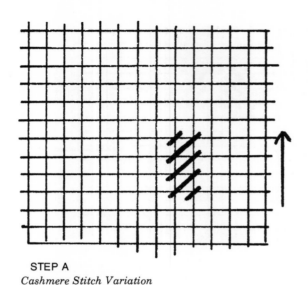

STEP A

Cashmere Stitch Variation

STEP B

Mosaic Stitch

Start at the bottom of the canvas and work all the rows from right to left. Turn the canvas upside down at the end of each row. Step B shows the first stitch of the next square. Step C shows the first stitch of the second row.

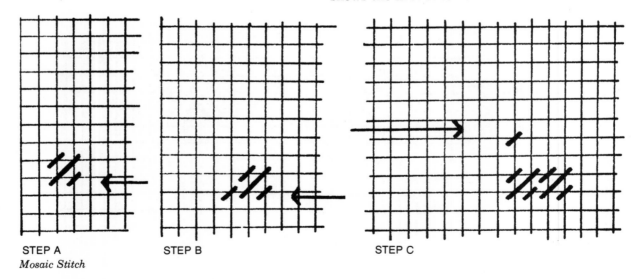

STEP A

Mosaic Stitch

STEP B

STEP C

Knotted Stitch

Start at the top of the canvas and work all the rows from right to left. Turn the canvas upside down at the end of each row. Step C shows the first stitch of the second row.

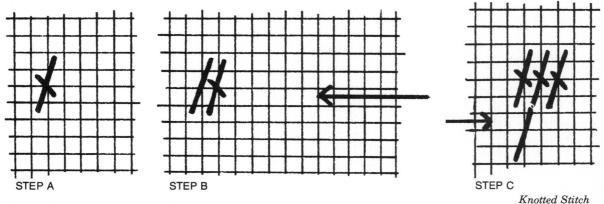

STEP A   STEP B   STEP C

Knotted Stitch

Fern Stitch

Work all the rows from the top to the bottom of the canvas. Step A shows the beginning of a row. Follow with step B and repeat step C for the stitch. Step D shows the end of the row. The arrow marks the beginning of the second row.

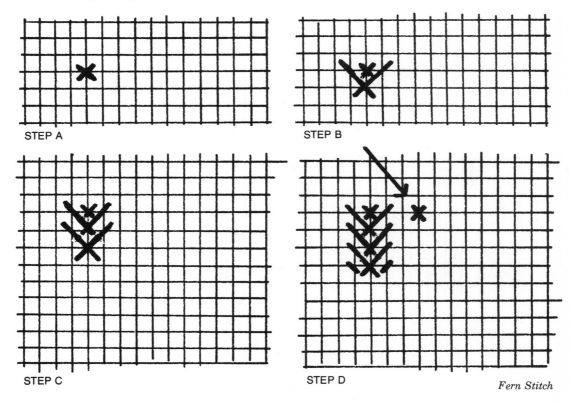

STEP A   STEP B

STEP C   STEP D

Fern Stitch

Florentine Stitch

This is the basic Bargello stitch. Each row can be worked in a different color. Start at the center of the canvas and work the first row from the center to the sides. Work the following rows up to the center of the canvas. Turn the canvas upside down and finish the other half.

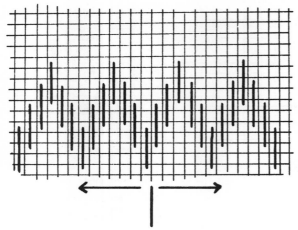

Florentine Stitch

Hungarian Stitch

Each row can be worked in a different color. Start at the top of the canvas. Work the first row from left to right and the second row from right to left.

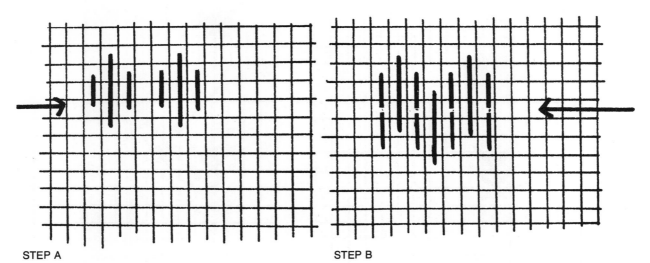

STEP A   STEP B

Hungarian Stitch

Leaf Stitch

The first row of leaves is done at the top of the canvas. Finish all the rows from left to right. Step B shows the first stitch of the second leaf. Step C shows the first stitch of the second row.

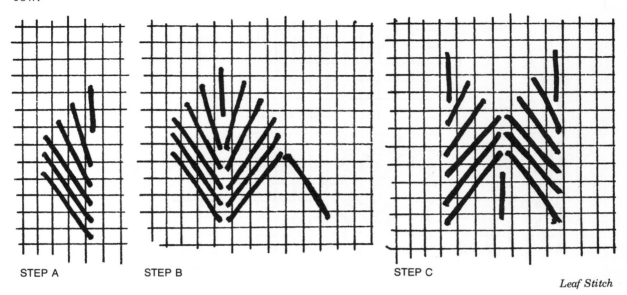

STEP A   STEP B   STEP C

Leaf Stitch

Long and Short Oblique Stitch

Start at the bottom left of the canvas. Work the first row from the bottom up and work the second row from the top down.

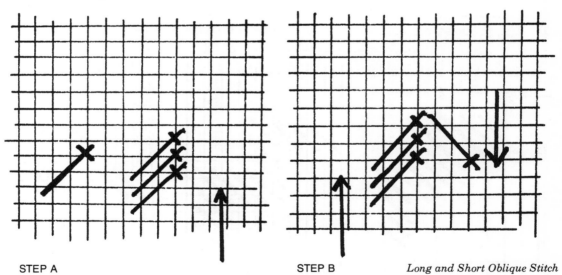

STEP A   STEP B   *Long and Short Oblique Stitch*

Stem Stitch

Work the first row from the bottom up. Work the second row from the top down. Steps A and B show the beginning and ending of the rows. Work a row of backstitches between each row of stem stitches with a lighter-weight yarn.

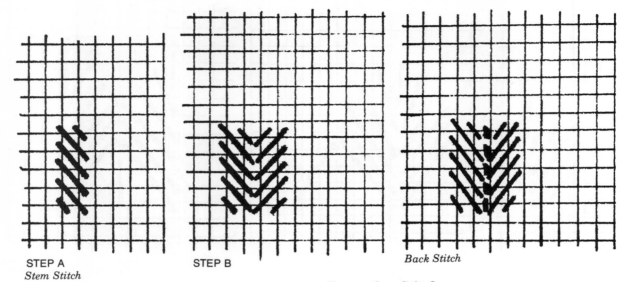

STEP A
Stem Stitch

STEP B

Back Stitch

Byzantine Stitch

The Byzantine stitch may be done in two colors. Start working at the bottom of the canvas. Step B shows the first stitch of the second row. Step C shows the continuation of the second row. When the first half of the work is finished, turn the canvas upside down to complete the other half.

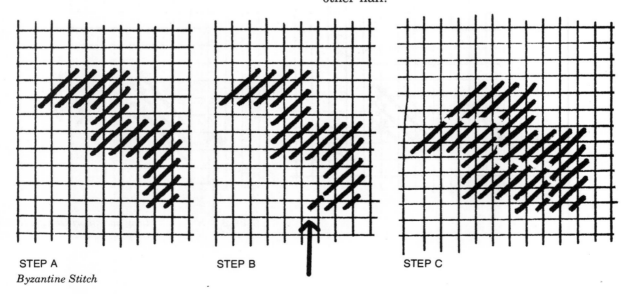

STEP A
Byzantine Stitch

STEP B

STEP C

Milanese Stitch

The Milanese stitch may be done with two different colors. Start working at the top left of the canvas. Turn the canvas upside down at the end of each row. Step B shows the first stitch of the second row. Finish the other side of the canvas in the same manner.

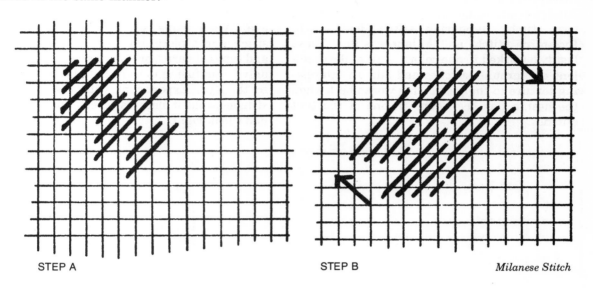

STEP A   STEP B   *Milanese Stitch*

Algerian Eyelet Stitch

The Algerian eyelet stitch can be worked over 1, 2, or 3 meshes of the canvas. Start by holding a short end of the yarn at the back of the canvas. Bring up the yarn to make a short stitch to the left. Continue as diagramed, radiating the stitches in a counterclockwise motion and bringing the yarn down through the same center hole. Step B shows a completed eyelet and the start of the next eyelet stitch to the right of the first one.

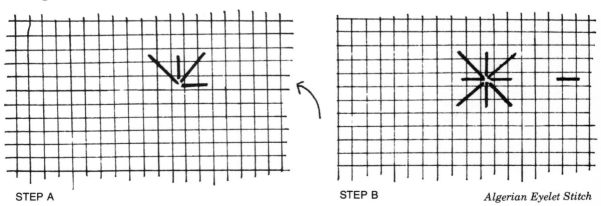

STEP A   STEP B   *Algerian Eyelet Stitch*

Using Decorative Stitches

Some of the previous decorative stitches — cross-stitch, upright cross-stitch, Long-legged cross-stitch, Smyrna cross-stitch, Scotch stitch, checkerboard stitch, cashmere stitch, cashmere stitch variation, mosaic stitch, knotted stitch, fern stitch, Hungarian stitch, leaf stitch, Byzantine stitch, and Milanese stitch (these last two worked in one color) — all make excellent background stitches and add an interesting texture to the piece. This works best when the design has been done in one of the tent stitches.

These and all the other decorative stitches can be incorporated into the design of the piece, but it is best to make a sampler first to see the effect of the stitch on the size of the canvas and in the kind of yarn you want to use. Plan projects using these stitches carefully beforehand, since too many different stitches on one piece of needlework can easily become too busy to the eye. When using several different kinds of stitches in a piece, limit the number of colors and types of yarns, or the finished piece will not only be confusing to work but also be confusing to the eye. Experiment with these different stitches, and if necessary, cut out those that don't look right.

4
Needlepoint Projects

Sampler Pillow (see photograph on the next page)

This pillow will serve two purposes. It will help you to learn and practice a number of different needlepoint stitches. And when you are finished, you will have a lovely decorative pillow, or if you wish, you can frame it.

What You Need

1 piece of 12-mesh canvas, 15 inches by 15 inches (the finished design is 12 inches by 12 inches)
½ yard backing fabric
½ yard muslin
Pillow stuffing
Persian yarn
    Ecru
    Light green
    Medium green
    Olive
    Navy

Mark off the canvas into 16 squares, each square having 30 threads with 2 rows between them for 2 rows of continental stitches. Follow the chart for the placement of the different stitches. The instructions for the individual stitches can be found on pages 23–38. Some of the squares require following the graphs given on these pages for the designs.

Square 1: Encroaching Gobelin stitch worked horizontally. Work the stitch in ecru and medium green.
Square 2: Algerian eyelet stitch worked in light green and olive. See the photograph.
Square 3: Byzantine stitch worked in light green and medium green.
Square 4: Hungarian stitch worked in light green and navy.

Sampler Pillow. Designed and worked by Ethel Nemeck.

SQUARE 1	SQUARE 2	SQUARE 3	SQUARE 4
SQUARE 5	SQUARE 6	SQUARE 7	SQUARE 8
SQUARE 9	SQUARE 10	SQUARE 11	SQUARE 12
SQUARE 13	SQUARE 14	SQUARE 15	SQUARE 16

Sampler Pillow

X = ONE CROSS-STITCH

Sampler Pillow   Square 8

Square 5: Checkerboard stitch worked in light green, medium green, and olive. See the photograph for placement.

Square 6: Florentine stitch flower worked in ecru, light green, medium green, olive, and navy. See the graph for color placement.

Square 7: Smyrna cross-stitch worked completely in light green.

Square 8: Triangle stitch worked in light green and medium green. See graph for color and stitch placement.

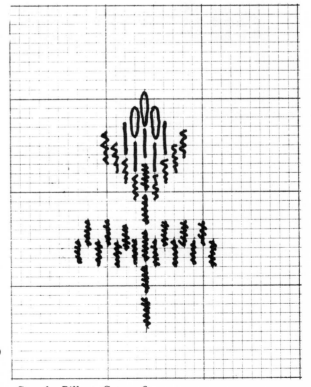

0 NAVY

| LIGHT GREEN

§ MEDIUM GREEN

‡ OLIVE

ECRU BACKGROUND

Sampler Pillow   Square 6

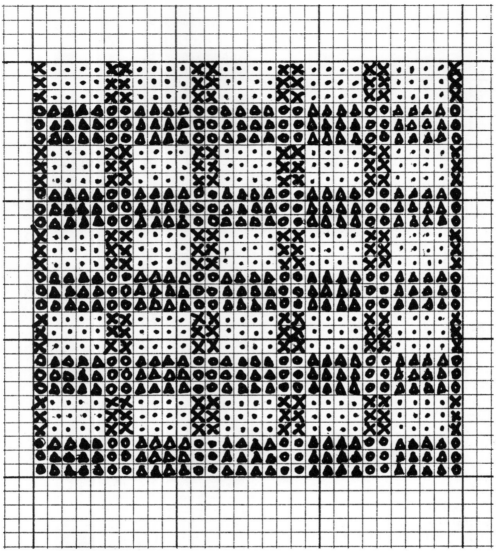

Sampler Pillow   Square 10

△ LIGHT GREEN

✕ MEDIUM GREEN

○ OLIVE

● ECRU

Square 9: Cross-stitch worked from top to bottom as follows: 2 rows of olive, 3 rows of medium green, 2 rows of light green, 3 rows of ecru, 2 rows of light green, three rows of medium green.

Square 10: Tent Stitch, plaid worked in ecru, olive, and light green. See graph for color placement.

Square 11: Detail worked in navy with ecru background. See page 78 for Alphabet.

Square 12: Milanese stitch worked from top to bottom in olive and ecru.

Square 13: Stem stitch worked without the backstitch mentioned on page 36. Work the colors from left to right as follows: medium green, ecru, navy, ecru, and medium green.

Square 14: Florentine stitch worked in light green, ecru, olive, and medium green. See graph for color placement.

Square 15: Tramé cross-stitch worked in light green with olive. One row of light-green continental stitch worked around the entire square.

Square 16: Byzantine Stitch worked over 2 and 1 threads alternatively. Starting in the upper right-hand corner, the color sequence is as follows: light green (worked over 2 threads), olive (worked over 1 thread), ecru (worked over 2 threads), and olive (worked over 1 thread). Repeat this sequence to the end of the square.

To make the border of the pillow, work 9 rows of continental stitches as follows: from the center out, 3 rows navy, 1 row medium green, 1 row ecru, 1 row medium green, 3 rows navy.

To make the pillow, follow the instructions on page 82 for a pillow with a piped edge.

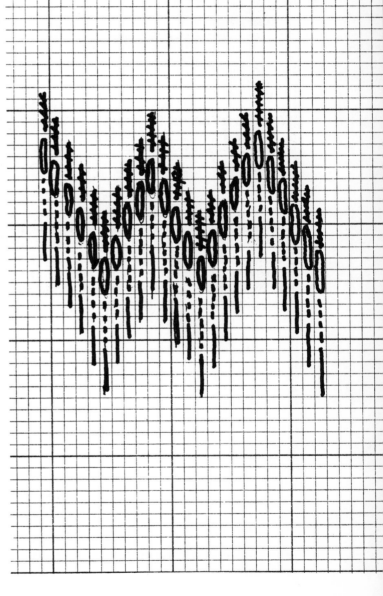

¦ LIGHT GREEN

O MEDIUM GREEN

‡ OLIVE

❙ ECRU

Sampler Pillow   Square 14

Bookmarks

These bookmarks are quick and easy to make. They are perfect for first projects, and you can use up little pieces of left-over canvas if you choose to make your first project more ambitious.

What You Need
1 piece of 12-mesh canvas, 12 inches by 4 inches, for each bookmark
1 piece of felt the same size in the same color as one of the yarns.
White glue
Tapestry yarn
Flowers with Berries Bookmark
    Yellow
    Red
    Green
    White

Flowers with Leaves Bookmark
    Yellow
    White
    Green
    Dark blue

After you have traced the design on the canvas, work the flowers with berry or leaf motifs. Then fill in the background. When the stitching is complete, block each bookmark as described on page 80. Finish the backs following the instructions given at the end of the next project, the Dollhouse Rug.

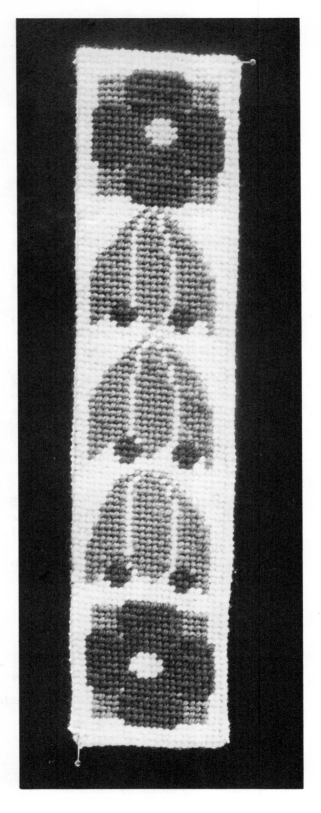

Bookmark – Flowers with Berries. Designed and worked by the author.

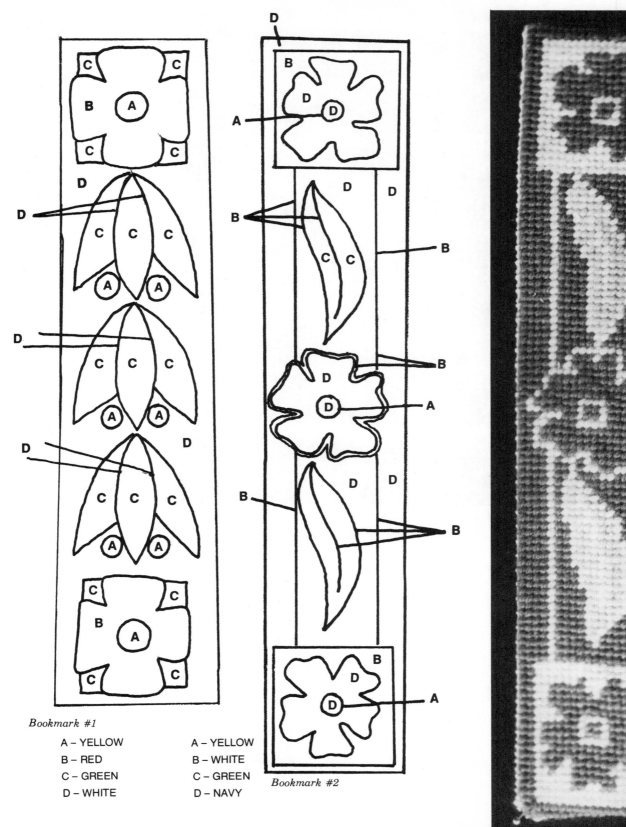

Bookmark #1

A – YELLOW	A – YELLOW
B – RED	B – WHITE
C – GREEN	C – GREEN
D – WHITE	D – NAVY

Bookmark #2

Bookmark – Flowers with Leaves. Designed and worked by the author.

Dollhouse Rug.   Designed and worked by the author.

Dollhouse Rug

This little rug is the perfect gift for any doll-house owner, young or old.

What You Need
1 piece of 12-mesh mono canvas, 7 inches by 7 inches
Felt
White glue
Persian yarn
   Dark red
   Beige
   Dark brown

Follow the graph for the placement of the colors.

After the rug has been blocked, cut the canvas as shown at each corner at a 45-degree angle. Fold the canvas to the back, creasing it along the last row of needlepoint stitches. Lay down a *light* coat of white glue under the canvas. Press the canvas down to glue it to the back of the stitching. After the glue has dried, cut out a piece of felt the same size as the finished rug. Glue the felt to the back of the rug, being careful not to use too much glue.

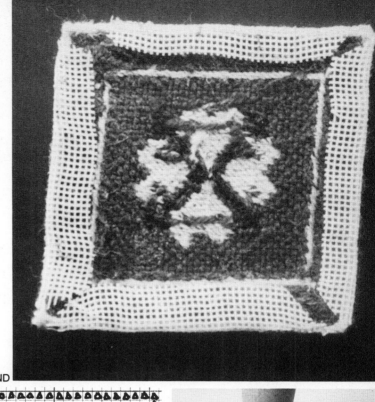

Piece with the canvas folded back and then glued down.

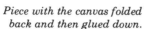

▲ BEIGE ✗ DARK BROWN   DARK RED BACKGROUND

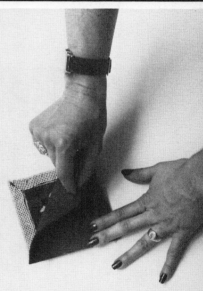

Gluing the felt to the back of the finished needlepoint.

Dollhouse Rug

Christmas Tree Ornaments

These Christmas tree ornaments are not only charming and easy to make, they have the great advantage of being unbreakable. You can either make several of them for your own tree or make one for each of your special friends and send them as completely personal Christmas cards.

What You Need
1 piece of 10-mesh mono canvas 6 inches by 6 inches for each ornament
Red or green felt
White glue
Tapestry yarn

Holly Ornament
   Light green
   Dark green
   Red
   White
   Gold metallic knitting yarn (sport weight)

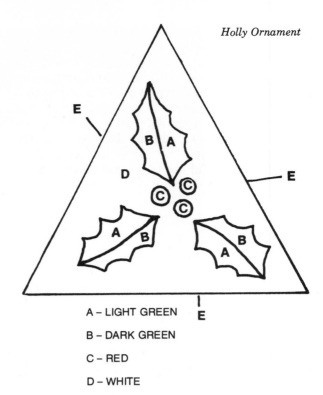

Holly Ornament

A – LIGHT GREEN

B – DARK GREEN

C – RED

D – WHITE

E – GOLD

Christmas Ornament – Holly.
Designed and worked by the author.

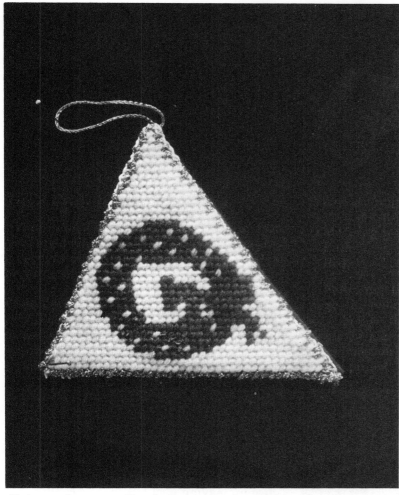

Christmas Ornament – Wreath. Designed and worked by the author.

A – DARK GREEN

B – WHITE

C – RED

D – YELLOW

E – BLUE

F – GOLD

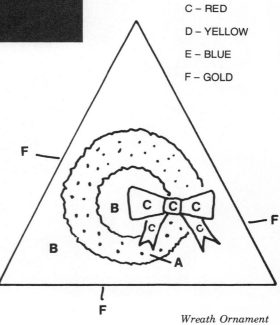

Wreath Ornament

Wreath Ornament
   Dark green
   Red
   Yellow
   Magenta
   White
   Gold metallic knitting yarn (sport weight)

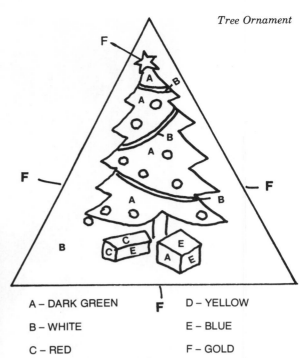

Tree Ornament

Tree Ornament
    Dark green
    White
    Red
    Yellow
    Blue
    Gold metallic knitting yarn (sport weight)

A – DARK GREEN   D – YELLOW

B – WHITE   E – BLUE

C – RED   F – GOLD

TREE ORNAMENTS: ALTERNATE COLORS B, C, D, & E

After the pieces have been blocked, trim off the canvas. Follow the triangular shape of the design, leaving about ⅝ inch of canvas all the way around. Make a clip at each point of the canvas, being careful not to cut the stitching. Fold the canvas under and glue it to the back of the needlepoint stitching. Make a loop out of a 5-inch piece of gold yarn and glue the end of it to the top of the ornament as shown. Cut out a piece of felt the same size as the finished piece. Glue the felt to the back of the ornament, being sure to cover the ends of the gold loop.

Christmas Ornament – Christmas Tree. Designed and worked by the author.

Coasters

These coasters work up very quickly, and you can make as many as you need from left-over canvas and yarn.

What You Need
1 piece of 12-mesh mono canvas 8 inches by 8 inches for each coaster
Felt
White glue
Persian yarn
Tulip Coaster
    Red
    White
    Light green
    Dark green

Tulip Coaster. Designed and worked by the author.

A – RED

B – WHITE

C – DARK GREEN

D – LIGHT GREEN

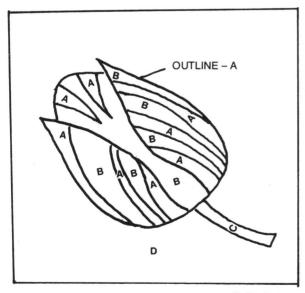

Tulip Coaster

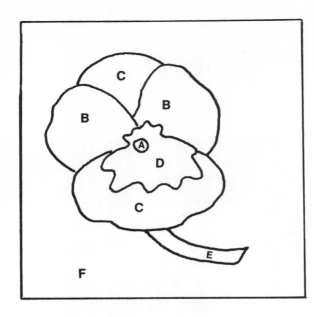

A – YELLOW

B – LIGHT PURPLE

C – MEDIUM PURPLE

D – DARK PURPLE

E – DARK GREEN

F – LIGHT GREEN

Pansy Coaster

Pansy Coaster
   Yellow
   Light purple
   Medium purple
   Dark purple
   Dark green
   Light green

Pansy Coaster. Designed and worked by the author.

Anemone Coaster
Red
White
Black
Dark green
Light green

Anemone Coaster. Designed and worked by the author.

A – RED

B – WHITE

C – BLACK

D – DARK GREEN

E – LIGHT GREEN

Trace the patterns and follow the key for color placement. Finish the blocked piece with the glue and felt as instructed in the Bookmarks project.

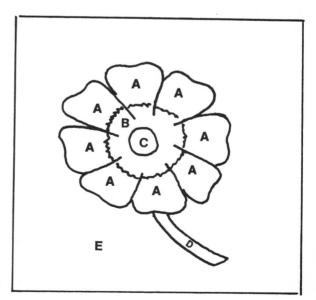

Anemone Coaster

Playing Card Pillow

This little pillow is ideal as a gift for your bridge-playing friends or as an accent in your den or game room.

What You Need
1 piece of 12-mesh canvas, 12 inches by 12 inches (the finished design is 9 inches by 9 inches)

Tapestry yarn
Peach   Red
Emerald green Black

The entire pillow is made in the tent stitch. Fold the canvas to find the center. Mark off triangles and then trace in the patterns. Follow the diagram for color and pattern placement. Block the canvas and make up into a pillow as instructed on pages 82–84.

A – PEACH   C – RED

B – EMERALD GREEN   D – BLACK

Playing Card Pillow. Designed and worked by Lydia Encinas.

Full-size Patterns for Playing Card Pillow

Art Deco Flower Bouquet Pillow

This lively design done in the Art Deco style of the thirties is a good choice for your first large project. Simply enlarge the design and trace it onto the canvas. It is not necessary to count stitches except for the purple border, which should be 9 stitches deep.

What You Need

1 piece of 12-mesh mono canvas — 18 inches by 18 inches (the finished design is 13 inches by 13 inches)

½ yard of velveteen or satin backing fabric

Pillow stuffing

½ yard muslin

Tapestry yarn

Shocking pink	Red
Magenta	Turquoise
Bright green	Light purple
Chartreuse	Dark purple
Orange	White
Yellow	Black

Follow the diagram for color placement. Make the flowers and vase first, then the background, and finally the border. When the piece has been blocked, follow the instructions on page 82 for making a knife-edge pillow.

Art Deco Flower Pillow. Designed and worked by the author.

A – SHOCKING PINK

B – MAGENTA

C – BRIGHT GREEN

D – CHARTREUSE

E – ORANGE

F – YELLOW

G – RED

H – TURQUOISE

I – LIGHT PURPLE

J – DARK PURPLE

K – WHITE

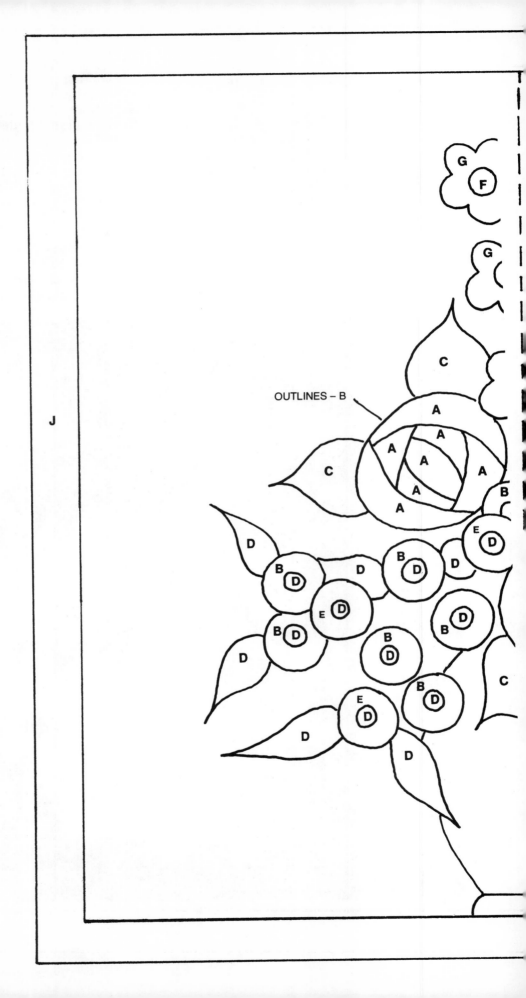

J

J

G
F

F

G
F

C

H
F

E
F → F

OUT-
LINES
B

A A
A A
A
A

C

F B

B C
C
C F C
C

H
F

C

E
F → F

D D C

A A
A
A A
A
A

H F

B

H
F

F

C

OUTLINE B

H
F

H

K

BLACK BACKGROUND

I

I

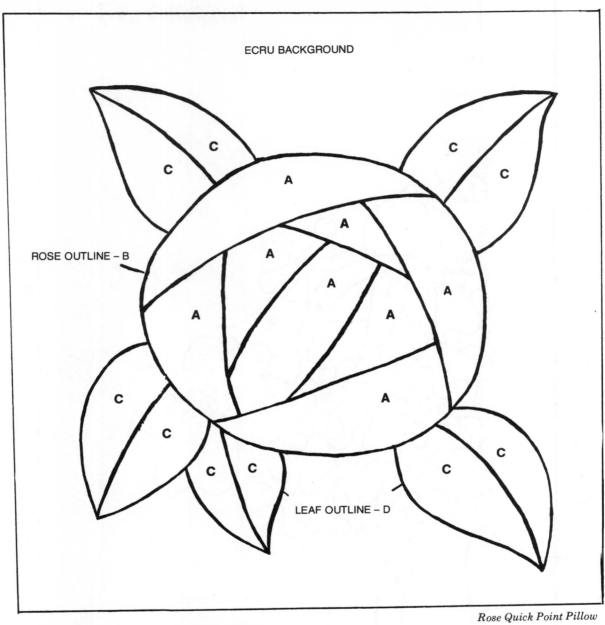

ECRU BACKGROUND

ROSE OUTLINE – B

LEAF OUTLINE – D

Rose Quick Point Pillow

A – PINK   C – LIGHT GREEN

B – RED   D – DARK GREEN

           ECRU

Rose Quick Point Pillow

This is an ideal project for children, teenagers and older people, since the large mesh of the canvas makes the stitches very easy to see the work quickly.

What You Need

1 piece of 4-mesh rug canvas, 16 inches by 16 inches (the finished design is 13½ inches by 13½ inches)
½ yard of velveteen backing fabric
Pillow stuffing
½ yard muslin

D.M.C. rug wool	
Pink	Light green
Red	Dark green
	Ecru

Following the square method described on page 18, enlarge the design to the required size. Follow the diagram for color placement. After the piece has been blocked, follow the instructions on pages 82 for making a knife-edged pillow.

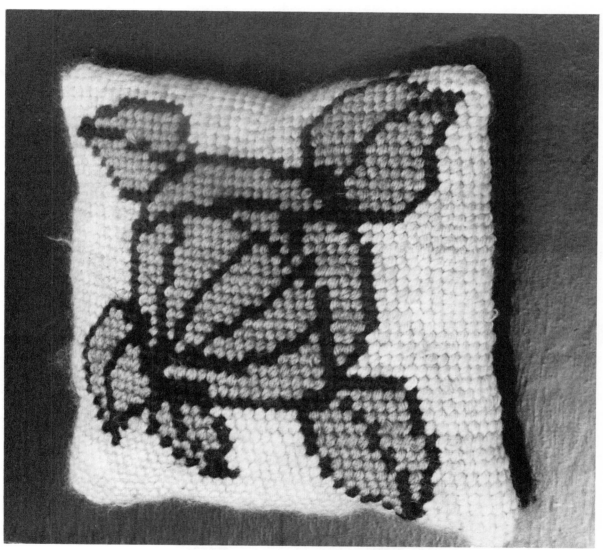

Rose Quickpoint Pillow. Designed and worked by the author.

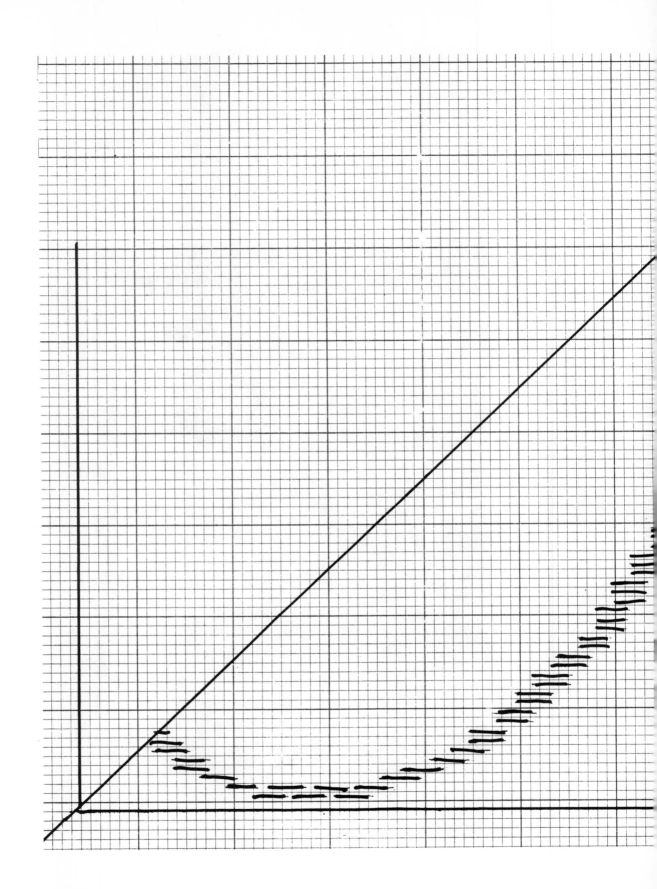

Four-way Bargello Pillow

After you have had some experience with other projects, you will be ready to make this beautiful Bargello pillow. It is called "four-way" because the canvas is divided into quarters and each quarter is worked in sections.

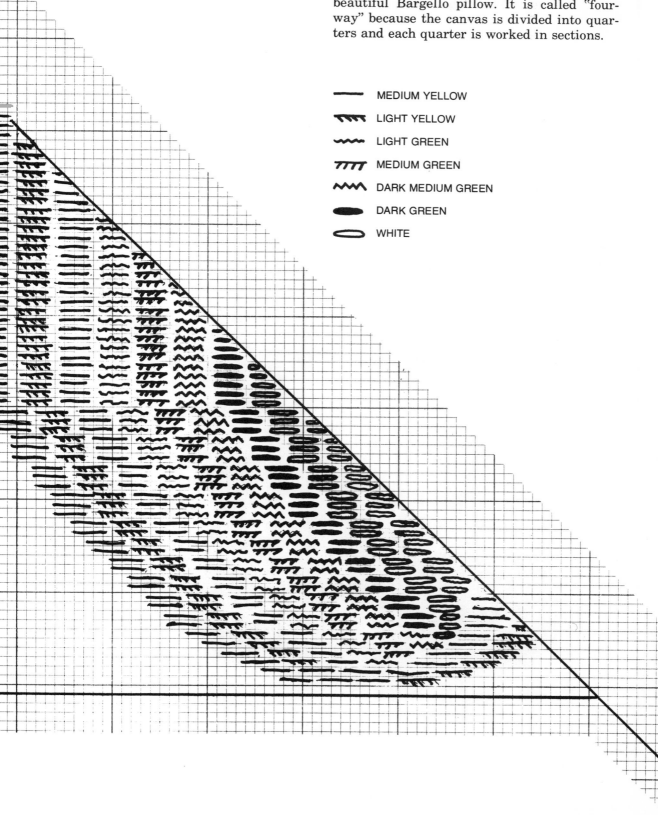

— MEDIUM YELLOW

LIGHT YELLOW

LIGHT GREEN

MEDIUM GREEN

DARK MEDIUM GREEN

DARK GREEN

WHITE

What You Need

1 piece of 13-mesh Bargello canvas, 14½ inches by 14½ inches (the finished design is 10½ inches by 10½ inches

½ yard of velveteen backing fabric

Pillow stuffing

½ yard muslin

Persian yarn

    Light yellow

    Medium yellow

    Light green

    Medium green

    Dark medium green

    Dark green

    White

Fold the canvas in half and in half again to determine the center of the canvas. Draw the center lines lightly on the canvas with a pencil. Use a ruler to draw a line that bisects the center lines at a 45-degree angle. Repeat this for the other side. Starting at the center of the canvas, use a Gobelin stitch that covers 4 meshes of the canvas. Make your first stitches with medium yellow yarn. Work one quarter of the canvas at a time. Follow the chart on page 63 for stitch and color placement. Once you have finished one quarter of the design, make the other three in the same way.

See pages 82–84 for instructions on making a pillow with a piped finish.

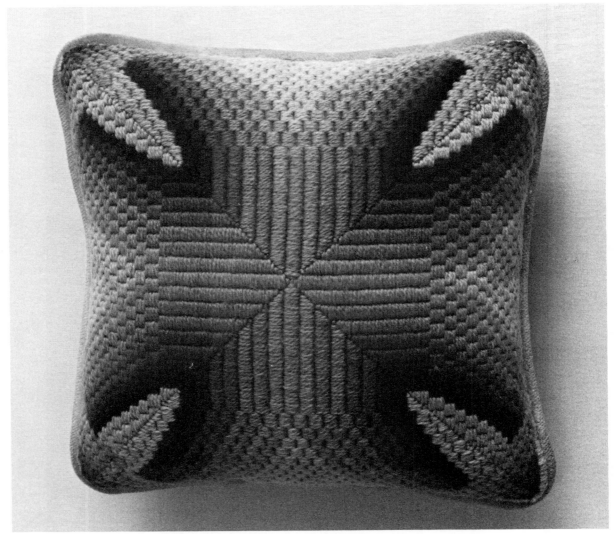

Four-way Bargello Pillow. Designed and worked by Barni Smith.

Paperback Book Cover. Designed and worked by the author.

Paperback Book Cover

This perky design will add a nice touch to any paperback book you read, since the cover can be taken off and used on many different books as long as they are of a similar size. With a slight alteration in the finished dimensions, the same design can be adapted to make a cover for television guides.

What You Need
1 piece of 10-mesh canvas, 8 inches by 10 inches (the finished design is 6 inches by 7½ inches)

Stiff cardboard, twice the size of the finished piece.

Felt

White glue

Tapestry yarn

Shocking pink	Light green
Magenta	Dark purple
Light orange	Light purple
Dark orange	Yellow
Medium green	Black

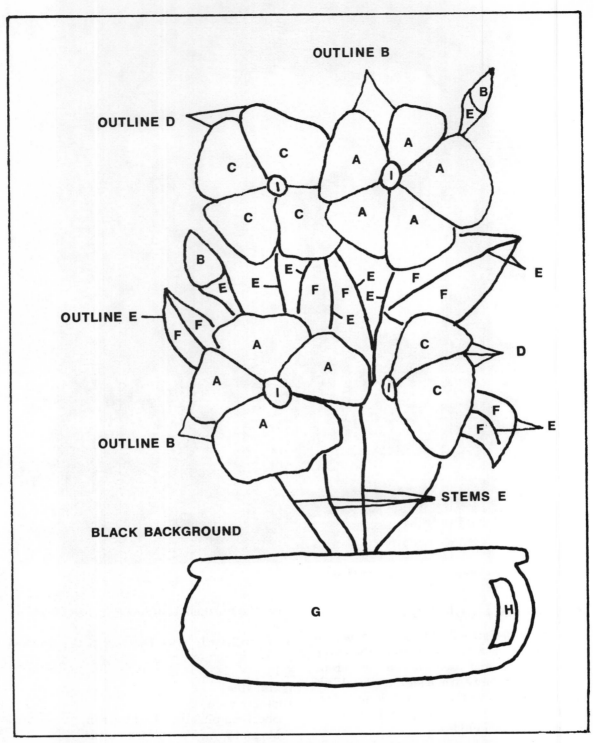

Color Placement Guide

A – SHOCKING PINK	D – DARK ORANGE	G – DARK PURPLE
B – MAGENTA	E – MEDIUM GREEN	H – LIGHT PURPLE
C – LIGHT ORANGE	F – LIGHT GREEN	I – YELLOW

Enlarge the design to the needed size by using the square method on page 18. Follow the diagram for color placement. After the piece is finished and blocked, trim the edges of the canvas to ⅝ inch all around. Make a clip in the right-hand corners. Fold the canvas to the inside and glue it to the back of the stitching. Cut 2 pieces of cardboard the size of the paperback book cover minus the spine of the book. Glue 1 piece of the cardboard to the back of the needlepoint. On the left-hand side, about an inch of needlepoint should stick out for the spine. Glue the second piece of cardboard to the unfinished canvas at the spine end of the book. Cut 3 pieces of felt the same size as the cardboard. Glue one piece to the cardboard on the back of the needlepoint. Glue the other 2 pieces so that they cover the cardboard on the back. Cut a strip of felt the width of the spine of the book and glue it to the back of the needlepoint at the spine. Cut 2 more strips of felt half the size of the cover. Glue the strip down to the inside of the book at the farthest ends, glueing the felt on 3 sides so that it forms a pocket (see illustration).

Back of the book cover with the cardboard glued to the right hand side. Note how the edges of the canvas have been folded and glued down.

Back of the book cover with the felt glued into place.

Inserting the book into the felt pockets on the inside.

Butterfly Picture

This beautiful butterfly makes a lovely pillow as well as a picture, as shown here. Framers can be found in the Yellow Pages, but call first to make sure that they are familiar with framing needlepoint (most of them are). You can have your needlepoint framed with or without glass. I prefer to leave the glass off, since this way the texture of the stitches can be more easily seen. If you decide to have a piece framed without glass, apply a protective spray after you have blocked it. If you follow the instructions on the can, your piece will probably never need cleaning. See pages 86–88 for instructions on framing needlepoint.

What You Need
1 piece of 10-mesh canvas, 15 inches by 19 inches (the finished design is 11 inches by 15 inches)
Tapestry yarn
    Navy
    Dark turquoise
    Medium turquoise
    Red
    Yellow
    White

Start the stitching with the navy outline of the butterfly's body, antennae, and wings. Fill in the solid areas of color in the wings and then work the background. If you want to make the butterfly into a pillow, see pages 82 for instructions for making a knife-edge pillow.

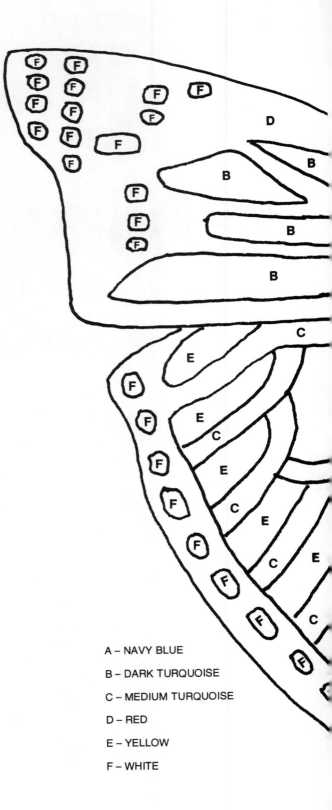

A – NAVY BLUE

B – DARK TURQUOISE

C – MEDIUM TURQUOISE

D – RED

E – YELLOW

F – WHITE

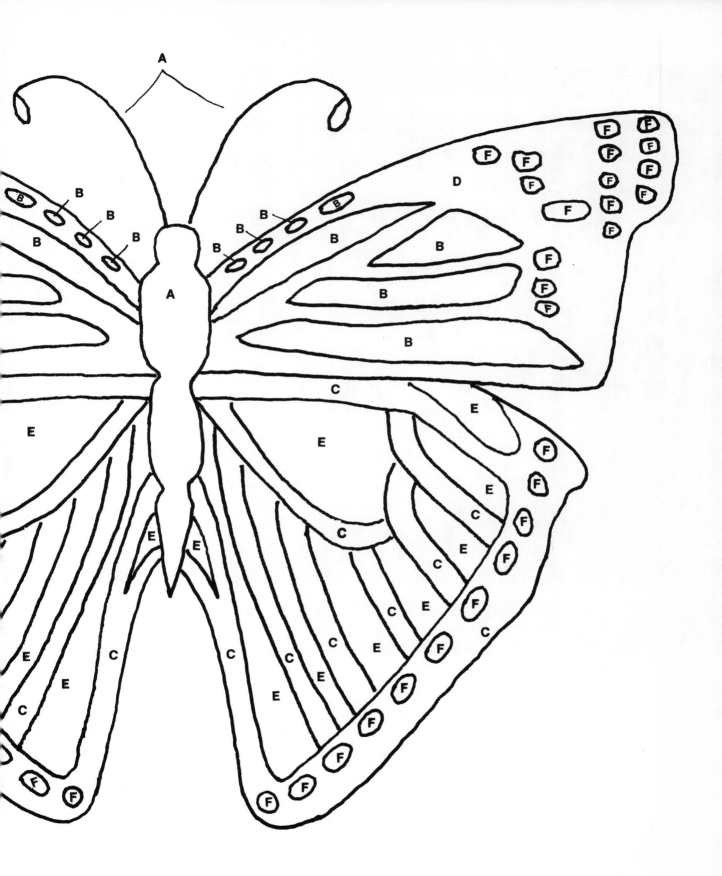

Butterfly Picture. Designed and worked by Barni Smith.

Floral Picture. Designed and worked by Barni Smith.

Floral Picture

This contemporary floral adds cheer to any decor.

What You Need
1 piece of 12-mesh canvas, 22 inches by 23 inches (the finished design is 18 inches by 19 inches)
Persian yarn

Olive green	Medium pink
Medium blue	Dark pink
Medium orange	Medium blue-green
Yellow	Navy
Red	Lavender
Dark red	White
Dark blue-green	

Follow the diagram for the color placement. After the piece has been blocked, have it framed or make it into a pillow following the instructions on pages 82–84.

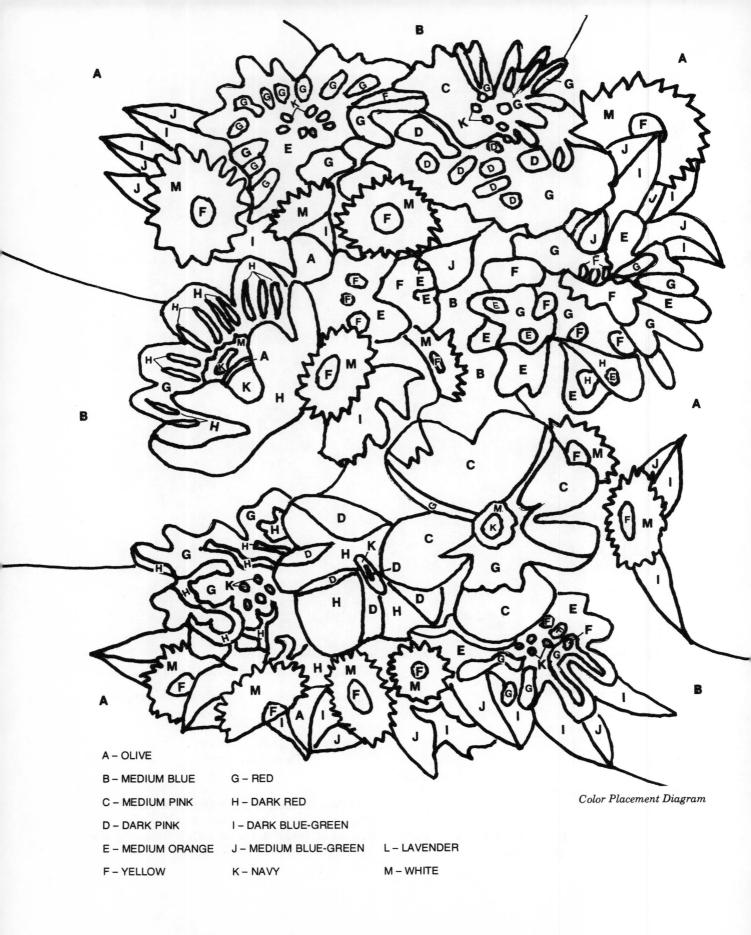

A – OLIVE

B – MEDIUM BLUE   G – RED

C – MEDIUM PINK   H – DARK RED

D – DARK PINK   I – DARK BLUE-GREEN

E – MEDIUM ORANGE   J – MEDIUM BLUE-GREEN   L – LAVENDER

F – YELLOW   K – NAVY   M – WHITE

Color Placement Diagram

Flame Stitch Bargello Pillow

This pillow is made with one of the easiest and most effective Bargello designs. Once you have laid in your basic line (as illustrated on p. 74) and have completed one or two of the motifs, you will find that the rest of the pillow works up very quickly.

What You Need
1 piece of 10-mesh mono canvas, 18 inches by 21 inches (the finished design is 14 inches by 17 inches)

½ yard backing fabric
½ yard muslin
Pillow stuffing
Persian yarn
    Dark red   Orange
    Rose   Pale pink

Starting at the center of the canvas, follow the chart for the placement and the color of stitches. Make the first row dark red. Then fill in the rest of the colors and repeat until the pillow is finished.

See page 82 for instructions on making a knife-edge pillow.

Flame Stitch Bargello Pillow. Designed and worked by Lydia Encinas.

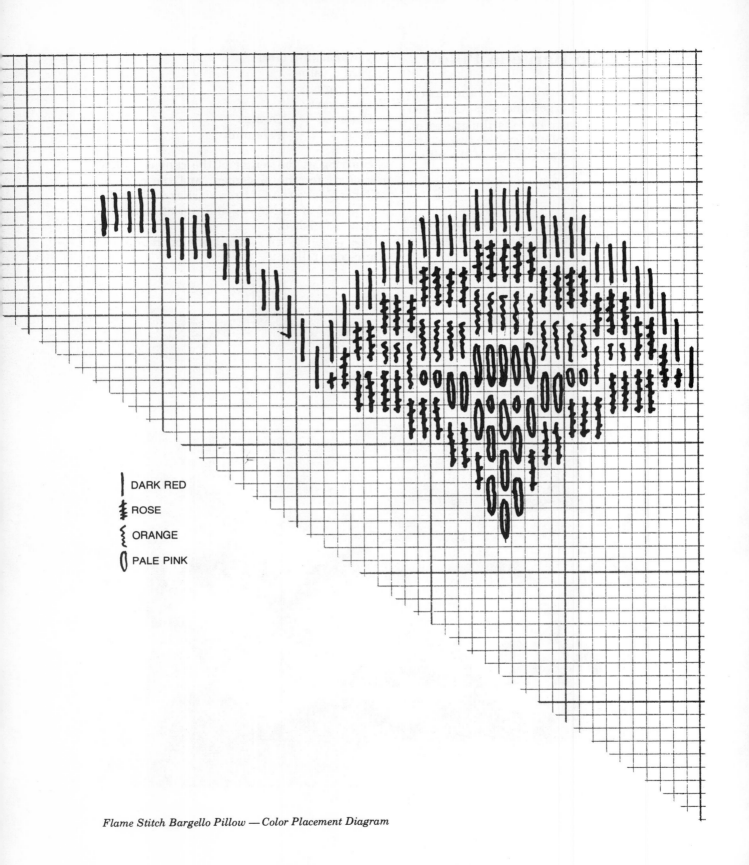

| DARK RED
‡ ROSE
§ ORANGE
(PALE PINK

Flame Stitch Bargello Pillow — Color Placement Diagram

Owls and Trees Picture. Designed and worked by Barni Smith.

Owls and Trees Picture

This is probably the most ambitious project in this book, but after completing a few of the other projects, you should be ready to make it. And your efforts will be well worth it! See the note at the beginning of the Butterfly Picture project about having needlepoint professionally framed.

What You Need

1 piece of 10-mesh canvas, 18 inches by 25 inches (the finished design is 14 inches by 21 inches)

Persian yarn
  Ecru
  Very light peach
  Medium peach
  Dark peach
  Very dark peach
  White
  Mustard gold
  Pale lavender
  Very pale lavender
  Medium blue-green
  Dark blue-green
  Light aqua
  Medium aqua
  Dark blue
  Red
  Yellow
  Brown
  Olive

Follow the diagram for color placement. When the picture is finished, block it and have it framed.

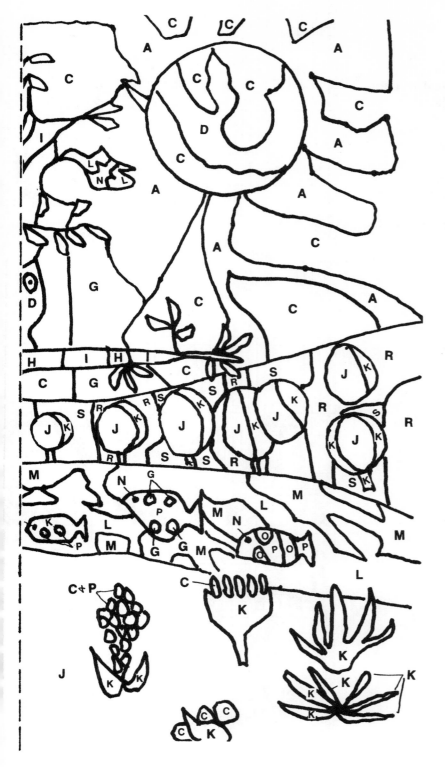

A – ECRU

B – VERY LIGHT PEACH

C – MEDIUM PEACH

D – DARK PEACH

E – VERY DARK PEACH

F – WHITE

G – MUSTARD GOLD

H – PALE LAVENDER

I – VERY PALE LAVENDER

J – MEDIUM BLUE-GREEN

K – DARK BLUE-GREEN

L – LIGHT AQUA

M – MEDIUM AQUA

N – NAVY

O – RED

P – YELLOW

Q – BROWN

R – OLIVE

S – LIGHT OLIVE

THE OWLS' EYES ARE WHITE
WITH NAVY CENTERS.

THE SMALL LEAVES ON THE LARGE
TREE ARE DARK BLUE-GREEN.

Alphabets

Here are graphs for alphabets in two sizes. You can use the smaller alphabet to initial your larger projects and to personalize gifts. Both alphabets can be used to needlepoint your favorite slogan on a pillow or picture.

When planning lettering for needlepoint, first work out the words on graph paper. This is necessary because different letters require a different number of stitches. Write out your slogan on the graph paper in pencil, making any necessary adjustments in the spacing.

Remember that the finished size of the slogan will depend on the size of the canvas mesh you are using, so plan your overall dimensions accordingly.

Alphabet Sampler

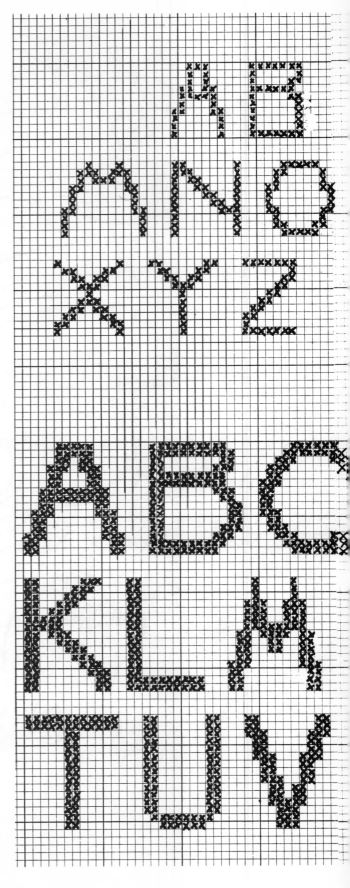

5
How to Finish Your Project

Blocking Needlepoint

Needlepoint must be blocked to restore the piece to a perfectly squared shape, since it will become slightly distorted as it is being stitched. The amount of distortion depends on the stitch used. A piece worked entirely in the continental stitch will probably be very out of shape, while one worked mainly in basketweave or Bargello stitches will require only a mild correction.

Use a waterproof marker and either a yardstick or artist's triangle to make 2 right angles on the plywood board mentioned at the beginning of this book. If the board gets dirty after several uses, you can extend its life by covering it with a piece of brown wrapping paper or clean unbleached muslin. Tack the paper or muslin over the entire board, getting it as flat as possible. Mark the right-angle lines on the paper or muslin as you first did on the board itself.

Take the piece of needlepoint, and if one edge of it is the selvedge of the canvas, make little clips in the selvedge along its length. Do not remove the masking tape. Place the canvas in *cold* water. When the canvas is thoroughly wet, gently press out some of the water. If the piece has been worked entirely in the tent stitch, place it on the board with the right side facing *down*. If it is a piece of Bargello, or if you have used any decorative stitches in the design, place the piece face *up* on the board. Line up the edges with the right-angle lines you have drawn. Tack the piece down along one side, spacing the tacks (be sure they are rustproof) about ½ inch apart.

Line up the adjacent side with the other line on the board, stretch the canvas tightly and tack it down as before. The amount of stretch needed depends on the amount of distortion in the canvas. Tack down the remaining sides, pulling the canvas as tightly as possible. (Don't worry, you can't tear a properly worked piece of needlepoint.)

Needlepoint pinned to blocking board. Notice that the right
side of the piece is facing the board.

Keep the canvas on the board for a few days and allow it to dry thoroughly. *Don't* try to hurry the process by placing it near a hot radiator or in direct sunlight. After the canvas is completely dry, remove it and check to see that the corners of the piece are at perfect right angles to each other. If the piece was very distorted to begin with, you may have to block it again. Simply repeat the entire process.

The only exception to the process described above is if you have used any silk thread in the work. If you have, take the piece to the board without wetting it at all. Once it is stretched and tacked to the board pass a steam iron over it. Don't let the iron lean on the canvas. Let the steam do the work.

If the work has become dirty while being worked, have it professionally dry cleaned before you block it, but be sure to tell the cleaner *not* to press it. If it is pressed during cleaning, it will be impossible to block properly.

Never attempt to wash needlepoint. The minerals in the water may react with the detergent or soap and you might wind up with a disaster. There are needlepoint cleaners on the market. Follow the instructions that come with the cleaners to clean mounted pictures or made-up pillows. If you apply a protective spray after you have finished blocking it, even a pillow worked in white should stay clean for years.

Making Pillows

Knife-edge Pillows

Make a pattern for the pillow the size of the finished needlepoint plus ⅝ inch for the back of the pillow. Using muslin, make an inner form for the pillow just a little smaller than the outside of the pillow. With the two pieces of muslin facing each other, sew around all the edges and corners. Leave a 4-inch opening in one side. Turn the muslin right-side out and stuff it with polyester or foam pillow stuffing. Sew the 4-inch opening together by hand. Stitch the backing fabric to the needlepoint in the same way, with the right sides of the needlepoint and the backing facing each other. Leave a 5-inch opening along one side. Turn the pillow right-side out through the opening, insert the muslin

form in the opening, and sew the opening together by hand.

Piped Pillows

Make an inner muslin form as described for knife-edge pillows. Cut bias strips of the backing fabric about an inch and a half wide and long enough to go around the edges of the finished needlepoint. Piece the strips where necessary. With the right side of the fabric facing you, fold the strip over a length of cording long enough to go around the edges of the needlepoint. With the right side of the needlepoint facing you, pin the piping around the edges of the needlepoint, raw edge facing the outer edges. Stitch in place. Place a piece of the backing fabric the same size as the finished needlepoint on top of the needlepoint, right sides facing each other. Stitch around the edges, sewing through the backing fabric, piping, and needlepoint. Leave a 5-inch opening along one edge. Turn the entire pillow right-side out, insert the muslin form, and sew the opening together by hand.

Square and Round Boxed Pillows

After the needlepoint has been finished and blocked, cut one piece of backing fabric the same size as the needlepoint top. Decide how wide you want the boxing strip to be. Cut a strip of the backing fabric the width of the boxing strip plus 1 inch for seam allowances and long enough to go around the top of the round or square pillow. Add 1 inch to the length for seam allowances.

Cut the bottom piece of the backing fabric in half and insert a zipper the length of the piece. Follow the instructions on the zipper package.

If you want your pillow to be piped or corded, follow the instructions for piped pillows. You will need twice as much cording for a boxed pillow as called for in the instructions for a piped, knife-edge pillow. Baste the cording to the right side of the needlepoint and the right side of the bottom piece of backing fabric.

Pin the boxing strip over the needlepoint (and over the cording if used). Join the edges of the strip. Stitch the joining and then stitch through the needlepoint, strip, and cording (if used). Open the zipper on the bottom and stitch

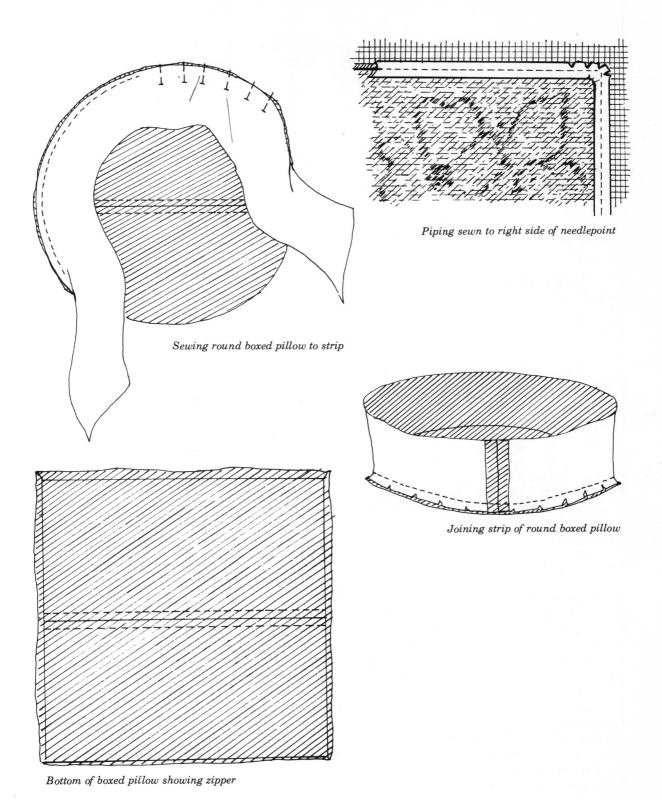

Piping sewn to right side of needlepoint

Sewing round boxed pillow to strip

Joining strip of round boxed pillow

Bottom of boxed pillow showing zipper

the bottom piece of fabric in the same way. Trim the seam allowances all the way around if your pillow is circular. Be sure that the clips don't cut into the stitching. Turn the pillow right-side out and stuff it through the open zipper. Don't skimp on the amount of stuffing you are using or your pillow will not have the firmness needed to show off the needlepoint to best advantage. When the pillow is nice and plump, close the zipper. Be careful not to catch the stuffing in the teeth of the zipper.

Making Chair Seats and Footstools

Needlepoint done in either the continental or basketweave stitch makes excellent covers for chair seats and footstools. When choosing a design for either, take into consideration the design of the piece of furniture and the decor of the room it will be in. Your choice can range from eighteenth- and nineteenth-century florals to striking modern geometrics. Check your local library for books of textiles and decorating for ideas. One word of caution: don't use a Bargello design for either a chair seat or a footstool; the long stitches of the Bargello work catch on things, and all your work may be ruined after just a few weeks of use. The best stitch for this purpose is the basketweave, since this stitch leaves a nice firm padding on the back of the work, which will literally wear for decades.

Because each chair seat and footstool is a slightly different size, take very accurate measurements before you draw out your needlepoint project. Footstools and many chair seats are slip seats. This means that the padded seat or top of the footstool slips out by means of screws and can be slipped back into place easily. Remove the seat before taking the measurements. Measure both the horizontal and vertical centers. If your chair seat has an irregular shape, follow the diagram to take the measurements. Be sure to allow for the depth of the padding. The needlepointed part of the canvas must cover the sides so that no unfinished canvas will show when the piece is attached to the chair seat or footstool. Add a

half inch in both directions, since the canvas will become slightly smaller as you work on it.

After you draw the design on the canvas (following the boundaries determined by the shape of the seat), add at least 2 inches of margin around the design. You will need these margins when you attach the needlepoint to the seat. After the needlepoint is finished, block the piece as described on pages 80–82. Trim the unfinished canvas around the edges, leaving an inch and a half all around. After the piece is trimmed, attach it to the seat with small upholstery tacks. Place the needlepoint over the seam and tack the opposite centers in place, pulling the needlepoint as tightly as possible. Tack all around the edges, placing the tacks about ¼ inch apart. You may find this procedure easier if you tape the trimmed edge of the needlepoint canvas with masking tape before you begin. This prevents the unworked canvas from unraveling as you work. Place the tacks just inside the tape and remove the tape after the piece is tacked into place.

You will need a piece of firmly woven cotton to finish the bottom of the seat. Measure it so that it covers the bottom of the seat, covering the raw edges of the needlepoint canvas plus ½ inch all around for seam allowances. Fold under the seam allowances and press them into place. Place the fabric over the bottom of the seat and tack it into place with upholstery tacks. Take several strands of each color of yarn you have used in the needlepoint and tuck them under the fabric. This way you will have them handy (and unfaded) should you have to make any repairs in the needlepoint cover.

Chair seats that are upholstered onto the wooden frame of the chair can also be replaced with new needlepoint covers. If the chair needs rebuilding or repairing, have this done first by a professional. Remove the original cover. You will have to make a muslin template of the seat before you plan your design. Cut the muslin to fit the chair seat. Allow a ½ inch in both directions for canvas shrinkage as you work. The front corners and back curves are not worked. After you are sure that your measurements are accurate, place the muslin on the needlepoint canvas and trace around the edges. Cut out the canvas in a square or rectangle. Leave at least 2 inches of canvas around the traced shape. Draw your needlepoint design within the traced lines. After the needlepoint has been worked, block the piece. Trim the canvas out of the front corners, leaving about ¾ inch. Using the background or predominant color, work a vertical continental stitch on the last thread of each side.

Center the design on the seat and fold under the unworked canvas. Using decorative upholstery tacks, tack the piece into place. Tack each side of the center first. Miter the unworked canvas at the front corners so that no unworked canvas shows. You will have to snip the back corners of the canvas and then fold them under. Once you have tacked the corners down, the fold at the back is hidden by the back of the chair. The same process can be followed for antique footstools that do not have tops that can be removed.

Making Boxes and Bricks

All kinds of small boxes can be covered with needlepoint. Bricks padded first with cotton batting or felt glued into place make original doorstops and bookends. Before you plan your needlepoint design, measure the box or brick carefully. The center rectangle is the top of the box or the brick. The four extensions will be folded down to cover the sides. The side extension pieces should be measured by counting the canvas meshes until you have achieved the measurement made with a ruler. This ensures that the sides will match exactly. Work the needlepoint and block the piece. Trim off the unworked canvas to within ¼ inch all around. Place a coating of white glue around the edges of the unworked canvas to keep them from unraveling. Turn the piece inside out and baste the corners together. Place the piece over the box top or brick and check the fit. Make any necessary adjustments. Machine stitch the corners in place. Lightly cover the seam with white glue to make sure that the seam won't open (remember that the white glue dries perfectly clear and won't show). Let the glue dry thoroughly.

Place the box top or brick in the needlepoint and glue the unworked canvas down. For boxes, line the inside of the top by gluing fabric or felt in place. For a brick, cover the unworked canvas by cutting out a piece of felt the size of the bottom of the brick and gluing it in place.

Making Belts

Belts can be made out of any size of canvas with a coordinating size and type of yarn. You can line the belt if you want to, but this is not absolutely necessary.

The first thing you must decide (after selecting the mesh size of the canvas) is the kind and size of the buckle you will use. Do this before you plan your design or cut the canvas. Many different kinds of buckles can be purchased in notion and button stores. You must allow a few extra inches in the length of the strip of canvas to allow you to attach the buckle. Not all belts require buckles. They can be closed with yarn loops, eyelets, or decorative hooks and eyes. Belts closed with hooks and eyes must be fitted more carefully than those made with loops or eyelets, which are fastened with an adjustable piece of yarn or a strip of leather.

Unlined Belts

Cut a strip of canvas the length of the finished belt and twice as wide. Fold the edges of the strip to the back and baste them together with ordinary sewing thread. Work the needlepoint on the front in a basketweave or continental stitch. Work through the two layers of canvas where it has been folded over. If the belt is pulled out of shape, block it before you do the edge stitch. Get the belt thoroughly wet. Attach the edge of the canvas to the blocking board with pushpins. Let the belt dry completely. Finish the long edges with a crossstitch.

Lined Belts

Mark off the measurements of your belt on the canvas. Tape the edges of the canvas with masking tape, leaving a 2-inch margin between the edges of the belt and the edge of the canvas. Work any needlepoint design you like, including Bargello. Block the canvas as described on pages 80–82. After the piece is completely dry, trim off the extra canvas to within ½ inch of the edge of the needlepoint. Turn the unworked canvas to the wrong side and glue it down with white glue. Get a firmly woven ribbon (preferably grosgrain) the width and length of the finished belt. Slip stitch it into place on the back of the belt with regular sewing thread.

Making Cylinder-shaped Projects

Cylindrical shapes can be used to cover wastebaskets, lamp bases, etc. The object you want to cover must have straight sides that do not slope, but you can cover oval or square-sided shapes. Choose an allover geometrical design or a Bargello design, since only part of the needlepoint will be seen from any one angle when the piece is attached to the object. Coordinate the size of the canvas mesh with the size of your object. A design made on a large-mesh canvas overwhelms a small pencil holder.

Measure the circumference and the height of the object accurately. Add ¼ inch to these measurements in each direction and you have the right size to draw on the canvas. Add seam allowances of 2 inches at each side and 1 inch at the top and bottom. Cut out the canvas along the seam allowances, edge them with white glue, and fold them to the back of the canvas. Baste the turned-in canvas in place with regular sewing thread, making sure that the canvas intersections match. Use masking tape to bind the two sides.

Work the needlepoint, going through both layers where the canvas is turned back. Leave 2 rows of canvas unworked at the top and bottom. Block the finished needlepoint and allow it to dry thoroughly. Check the fit of the canvas around the object. If it is too small, fill in the 4 rows of unworked canvas. If it is too large, you will have to take out as many rows as needed to make it fit.

Glue the piece to the object, making the ends meet. They may have to overlap a little. Cover the joining by gluing a piece of ribbon or decorative braid into place.

Framing Needlepoint

Most professional picture framers are equipped to frame needlepoint, but if you can buy a ready-made frame the size of your finished piece you can frame it yourself. Be sure that the frame you buy is *exactly* the same size as the finished needlepoint. If you want to frame it yourself and can't find a frame with the measurements you need, you can have one custom-made. This is almost as expensive as having a framer do all the work.

Whether you do the work yourself or have it done, be very selective in choosing the style of the frame. Take into consideration the style, size, and colors used in the needlepoint design. Remember the decor of the room in which the piece will hang. An extremely modern frame will look out of place in a period room, and vice versa. Also, don't forget the size of the room. A large elaborate frame may look beautiful with your needlepoint and look fine in the store, but if it overwhelms the room in which it hangs, you will spoil the whole effect. In general, the best frames for needlepoint are the simplest. An overly-busy frame will distract from the beauty of the needlepoint, and you want people to notice the needlepoint first, not the frame.

Frame the needlepoint without glass. A good protective spray will keep even the palest colors clean indefinitely. If you have used good-quality modern yarns, you needn't worry about the colors fading either. So don't let anyone tell you that you need the glass to keep the piece clean or to prevent fading or discoloration of the yarn. Glass obscures the texture of the stitch, and for work done in wool, there is another problem. All woolen yarn contains a certain amount of moisture. Sealed behind glass, this moisture can condense on the glass which means that you may have to remove the glass anyway and have the entire framing redone without it.

Before you can frame any piece of needlepoint, block it completely so that the original threads of the canvas are absolutely square. You may have to block the piece several times before it is ready for framing. Some, though not all, professional framers are expert at blocking needlepoint. Before you choose a framer, be sure that he has had a lot of experience working with needlepoint.

If you are going to frame it yourself, the first thing you need is a board to mount the needlepoint on. Use heavy cardboard or Masonite. Plywood can be used for small pieces which will sit on a table, but it is too heavy to hang up. Cut the board the same shape as the needlepoint but a fraction of an inch smaller than the piece. The needlepoint will be folded over the board with one or two rows of the stitching covering the edge of the board, so measure the board exactly.

Remove the masking tape from the needlepoint, if you have not already done so in the blocking process, but don't cut away any of the unworked margin. Sew bias tape around all four edges of the canvas. Be sure that the tape is strong and that it catches all of the threads of the canvas securely when it is sewn on. Cut off the corners of the canvas to form miters. Place the mounting board in the center of the piece and tape the sides down with masking tape. Be sure that enough needlepoint stitches cover the corners of the board to prevent the unworked canvas from showing or unraveling. Make sure that the board is centered perfectly. If necessary, keep moving the board until it is perfect. When it is absolutely right, use the masking tape to hold it securely.

Fold in one edge of the corner, fold the other one in and place it over the first one. Sew the corner in place with a tapestry needle and carpet thread. Sew through the folded edges of the corner with a running stitch and then whip stitch the edges together. Repeat for the opposite corner and then do the remaining corners. Remove the masking tape.

Now you have to lace the canvas across the board. Using carpet thread, start at the center and lace the canvas horizontally. Sew through the bias tape. Repeat these steps to lace it vertically. To make the lacing easier, thread the needle with the carpet thread but don't cut the thread. Make long stitches about a ¼ inch apart, pulling the canvas as tight as possible and letting the thread unwind from the spool as you work. When the horizontal lacing is finished, tie off the thread in a knot at the back of the work. Be careful not to let the lacing

BACK OF NEEDLEPOINT

Canvas primed for mitering

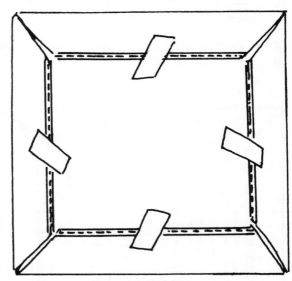

Corners mitered with sides taped down

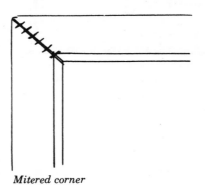

Mitered corner

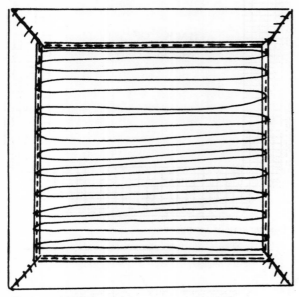

Horizontal lacing

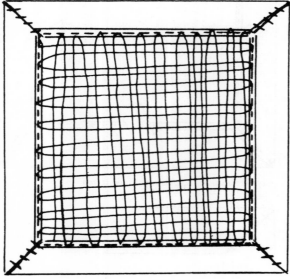

Horizontal and vertical lacing

stitches loosen. Repeat for the vertical lacing. The piece is now ready to be framed.

Slip the mounted needlepoint into the frame, wedging it into place. If it is a little loose, tack it to the frame with one or two headless nails.

The framed needlepoint will need a piece of backing paper to give it a professionally finished look. Buy a sheet of heavy brown paper at a stationery or art supply store. Don't use cutup grocery bags; they are not heavy enough. Cut the paper the size of the back of the frame, just within the edge. Place white glue along the edge of the brown paper. Place one edge of the paper along the edge of the frame, and working from the center out, press the glued edges of the paper in place. Make sure that the paper is perfectly smooth. Let the glue dry completely and then sprinkle the paper with cool water, getting it thoroughly damp but not soaking wet. The paper will shrink slightly as it dries, forming a tight covering. After the paper has dried attach the hardwear for hanging the frame. The glued paper backing will last indefinitely unless it gets torn, in which case it is easily replaced.

Making Rugs

Once you have finished several small needlepoint projects you will probably be in the mood to tackle something really impressive. The best way to do this is by making a rug. Needlepointing a rug is not difficult; it just takes longer than making a pillow, But the results are well worth the time spent.

Pieced Rugs

One of the easiest ways to make a beautiful rug is to make several squares, each 12 or 14 inches square. You can use the same design for each square and make the rug as large as you want by the number of squares you make. You can even make one additional square into a matching pillow. There are two advantages in using the pieced method. The first is that you are not restricted in the size of the finished rug by the available canvas widths. The second is that you can carry pillow-sized squares with you.

Once you have decided how large you want

your rug to be, divide the overall measurements by 16 or 18 inches square (this allows 4 inches for margins) to determine how much canvas you will need. By the way, just because you are making a rug, do not restrict yourself to rug-mesh canvas. Some of the most attractive needlepoint rugs are made on 10- or 12-mesh canvas.

Buy all of your canvas at the same time, and make sure that it all comes off the same roll. The weave of canvas differs slightly from bolt to bolt, and by buying it this way, you guarantee that the mesh of all the squares will be identical. Figure out how much yarn you will need and buy that at the same time also. Make sure that the colors all come from the same dye lot. You also will need rug binding and fabric tape.

Prepare each square as you would for a pillow, work the needlepoint, and block each square separately. Remove the masking tape and machine stitch around the edges of the unworked canvas to keep it from unraveling. Pin the squares together and sew them in strips first. Put a zipper foot on the machine so that you can sew as close to the needlepoint stitches as possible. Be sure that the design of the needlepoint squares all face in the same direction. When you have made as many strips as you need, match the seams and sew them together. Bind each raw edge with fabric tape on the back.

Stitch rug binding around the finished rug on the outer edges of the canvas. Turn the unworked canvas to the wrong side and whip stitch in place with carpet thread. Be sure that none of the unworked canvas shows on the right side.

One-piece Rugs

The width of your rug is determined by the width of the canvas, which usually comes in 36-, 40-, and 60-inch widths. When you plan your rug design, remember to allow for a 2-inch margin on each side and at the top and bottom. The length of the rug is determined by the yardage of the canvas.

Prepare the edges of the canvas with masking tape as you would for any other needlepoint project. Draw or paint your design on the can-

vas. You may want to invest in a large standing frame to work on, but it is not absolutely necessary. Buy all the yarn you need at one time to avoid dye-lot problems. Work as you would any needlepoint, but use only the basketweave. Any other stitch will cause an uncorrectable distortion of the canvas. You may have to use vertical or horizontal continental stitches for the design, but do not use the continental stitch for large areas or backgrounds.

As you work on the rug, steam it with an iron to keep the threads of the canvas as square as possible. Do not lean the full weight of the iron on the stitching — let the steam do the work.

Even if you steam the rug as you go along, you will have to block it to make it lie perfectly rectangular when finished. You can have the rug blocked professionally by a needlework shop or you can do it yourself.

Clip the selvedges of the canvas. Make ½-inch clips about an inch apart. You will need a board or stretcher 4 inches wider and 4 inches longer than your rug. Don't dampen the rug before you block it. Tack the four corners of the rug to the board or stretcher. Then tack the edges of the rug down, starting at the center of each side. You can also use a heavy-duty staple gun. Be sure that the tacks or staples go through the unworked canvas and not the needlepoint itself. Place the tacks about 1 inch apart, working toward the corners. Steam out any stubborn areas with a steam iron. Replace the tacks at the corners if the length of the edge makes a little bump when place the last few tacks before reaching the corner. When the rug has been completely tacked down, it should be as tight as possible.

Now dampen the rug thoroughly and leave it to dry completely. Remove the rug and check it. If it is still slightly off grain, you will have to block it a second time.

Miter the corners of the unworked canvas (see page 87). Fold in the side pieces and press them into place before sewing them. Then sew the long edges of the unworked canvas in place with carpet thread and a tapestry needle. Use a backstitch to sew the sides, being sure that no unworked canvas shows from the right side.

To bind the edge of the rug, thread a large rug needle (size #13) with as many strands of

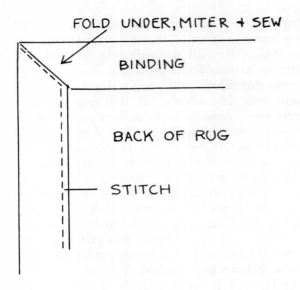

FOLD UNDER, MITER + SEW

BINDING

BACK OF RUG

STITCH

yarn as you can get through the eye of the needle comfortably. Start the binding at one of the corners of the rug. Take a few backstitches in the canvas hem of the rug and whip stitch along the edge of the rug. Make the stitches from the right to the wrong side, holding the rug with the edge and wrong side toward you. The stitches will cover the last row of the needlepoint stitches and the first row of the unworked canvas on the wrong side. Keep the stitching even, preventing the yarn from twisting. This will make a neat, rolled edge. When you come to within a few inches of the end of the yarn, weave it into the stitching at the back. Start the next strand by weaving a few inches under the stitches at the back. Be sure not to pull the yarn too tightly or the edge will form an unwanted ripple.

Lining

Both pieced and one-piece rugs can be lined. Get a piece of heavy cotton in a neutral color. You will need enough to cover the bottom of the rug plus 4 inches in each direction (you will have to piece it if the rug is wider than the fabric). Cut the fabric 4 inches wider and longer than the finished rug. Fold under 2 inches all the way around and miter the corners. Place the cotton on the back of the rug with the wrong sides facing. Pin the folded edge of the lining to the rug binding or whip stitching. Tack the lining to the center of the rug with long stitches. Catch stitch the folded edge of the lining to the rug binding or whip stitching.

Glossary

Bargello. A form of needlework done on needlepoint canvas with needlepoint yarns. The name refers to a castle in Italy where this style of needlework first became popular, having been brought to Italy from Hungary. The basic stitch for Bargello, called Florentine, is very simple. The changes in the colors of the yarn form the unique Bargello patterns.

Blocking. A method of stretching needlepoint work after it is finished in order to return the canvas to its original shape and to make all the stitches appear even. Instructions for blocking your needlepoint are on page 80, or you can have it done professionally by stores that specialize in needlepoint or by picture framers who are familiar with needlepoint.

Canvas. The stiff fabric on which needlepoint is done. It is usually made of cotton woven in perfectly even squares with holes left in between the threads. Each hole is referred to as a mesh, and the number of meshes to the inch determines the size of the finished design.

MONO CANVAS. Mono canvas is woven with 1 thread going in each direction. It is the most popularly used canvas today, since it is very easy to see the meshes for counting and stitching.

PENELOPE OR DUO CANVAS. Penelope or duo canvas is woven with 2 threads going in each direction. The threads can be separated in order to make two different-sized stitches on the same piece of canvas.

Decorative stitches. All stitches used for needlepoint that are not tent stitches. This includes the stitches used for Bargello work. Decorative stitches are great fun to experiment with, but they should not be attempted until the various tent stitches have been mastered.

Frames. This refers to the frames on which the needlepoint is worked, not picture frames used to frame a finished piece of work.

Graphs. Many needlepoint designs are worked from graphs. Each square of the graph represents a tent stitch, and the squares are usually marked with symbols standing for the various colors used in the design.

Needlepoint. Needlepoint has become a catch-all term to refer to any embroidery done on canvas. More specifically, needlepoint refers to work done in one of the tent stitches.

Persian yarn. A 3-ply yarn with a slightly hairy texture developed for use with needlepoint. It was originally meant to imitate the wool used for Persian rugs, and most of the colors imitate those used in Oriental rugs. It is one of the most popular needlepoint yarns, since the plys can be separated and used individually for fine details on small-mesh canvas.

Skeins. Yarn sold in lengths of 5 yards or more which has been wrapped up and labeled by the manufacturer. Skeins of yarn used for needlepoint must be cut into 18-inch strands before being used.

Tapestry. For many years, needlepoint or canvas work was referred to as tapestry work. It still is in Europe. Although real tapestries are woven and not embroidered, the confusion was brought about because the first needlepoint work done in Europe was made to imitate the more expensive and elaborate tapestry work.

Tapestry needles. In keeping with the confusion between the words "tapestry" and "needlepoint," needles used for needlepoint are still called tapestry needles. They differ from regular sewing needles in that they are thicker, have blunt tips, and have eyes large enough to accommodate woolen yarns.

Tapestry yarn. Tapestry yarn was developed in the beginning of the twentieth century for needlepoint work. It is a firmly twisted yarn without the hairiness of Persian yarn. The plies of tapestry yarn cannot be separated as they can be with Persian yarn, so tapestry yarn is most suitable for the larger-mesh canvases.

Tent stitch. There are actually four variations of the tent stitch (see pages 23–25). They all have the same appearance from the front of the work, that of a slanted stitch covering one intersection of the threads of the canvas. Because most modern needlepoint is done entirely in the tent stitch, these stitches are also referred to as the needlepoint stitch.

Tramé: Long, loose, horizontal stitch worked on the canvas in different colors. These stitches are covered with a tent stitch in the same color as the tramé. Many canvases imported from Europe have the design worked in tramé. These canvases are more expensive than printed or painted ones, since the tramé has been worked by hand. The tramé stitch adds strength to the finished canvas, although this is not necessary if the piece is worked in the basketweave or continental stitch.

Mail-order Supply Houses

Canvas, frames, tapestry and Persian wools, and other needlepoint supplies can be ordered by mail from these stores. If you write to them they will send you free catalogs. Buying from these stores can be the most economical way to buy supplies, since most of them offer a reduction in price for large orders.

Lee Wards
1200 St. Charles Road
Elgin, Illinois 60120

Merribee
P.O. Box 9680
Fort Worth, Texas 76107

Herrschners
Stevens Point, Wisconsin, 54481

D.M.C. Corporation
107 Trumbull Street
Elizabeth, New Jersey 07206

INDEX